Intuition of Significance

Intuition of Significance
Evidence against Materialism and for God

Albert Norton Jr.

RESOURCE *Publications* • Eugene, Oregon

INTUITION OF SIGNIFICANCE
Evidence against Materialism and for God

Copyright © 2019 Albert Norton Jr. All rights reserved. Except for brief quotations in critical publications or reviews, no part of this book may be reproduced in any manner without prior written permission from the publisher. Write: Permissions, Wipf and Stock Publishers, 199 W. 8th Ave., Suite 3, Eugene, OR 97401.

Resource Publications
An Imprint of Wipf and Stock Publishers
199 W. 8th Ave., Suite 3
Eugene, OR 97401

www.wipfandstock.com

PAPERBACK ISBN: 978-1-7252-5596-8
HARDCOVER ISBN: 978-1-7252-5597-5
EBOOK ISBN: 978-1-7252-5598-2

Scripture quotations are from The ESV® Bible (The Holy Bible, English Standard Version®), copyright © 2001 by Crossway, a publishing ministry of Good News Publishers. Used by permission. All rights reserved.

Manufactured in the U.S.A.   02/03/20

Contents

Introduction | vii

Chapter 1: The Question | 1
Chapter 2: Intuition | 10
Chapter 3: Existence of Physical Things | 14
Chapter 4: Nature | 19
Chapter 5: Ideals | 27
Chapter 6: Order | 32
Chapter 7: Disorder | 40
Chapter 8: History | 48
Chapter 9: Desire for Freedom | 60
Chapter 10: Conscience | 67
Chapter 11: Truth and Rationality | 81
Chapter 12: Consciousness | 89
Chapter 13: Knowledge, Belief, Faith | 101
Chapter 14: Significance | 110
Chapter 15: Yearning | 114
Chapter 16: Beauty | 120
Chapter 17: Gratitude | 123
Chapter 18: Religion | 126
Chapter 19: Silence | 142

See to it that no one takes you captive by philosophy and empty deceit, according to human tradition, according to the elemental spirits of the world, and not according to Christ.

—Colossians 2:8 ESV

Introduction

WHAT DOES A PERSON mean when he says, "I'm not religious?" We infer he has no strong pull toward the institutions of religion, or a compelling subjective motivation toward seeking spiritual truth. But note how the idea is typically phrased. It's apt to be an expression of what one *doesn't* believe; not what one does. This is routinely the way we think. In fact, this way of thinking is implicit in how we formulate the biggest question of all: Is there a God? "Yes" means yes, but "no" is only a negation of the theist proposition. One can answer "no" and be left with an illusory sense of neutrality concerning ultimate reality.

The average person, "religious" or not, is unlikely to have a reliable grasp on what the default metaphysical view in the culture teaches about ultimate reality. It takes some study and understanding, precisely because it is so typical of us to self-identify in reference to religion. Westerners who reject religion often don't make an effort to identify what metaphysical assumptions about ultimate reality they have taken up in its place. The false sense of neutrality devolves to materialism because the law, the culture, and our institutions drive us inexorably toward the materialist presumption.

Materialism is the idea that matter and the physical forces acting on it are all there is. Philosophers sometimes use the word "naturalism" for the same idea applied in a slightly different context: to say that all we experience occurs naturally; that is, without divine or supernatural intervention of any kind. We tend not to recognize the default metaphysical perspective as being coherent, doctrinal, and dogmatic, in the same way religion is understood to be. Like theism, however, materialism is a doctrine about the scope of all of reality. As such, it must on its own explain the evidence, including the evidence of our physical surroundings and our subjective appreciation of them.

There is a big gap between the theistic understanding of reality, and that of the default materialism of the culture. All variants of materialism are fundamentally in opposition to all variants of theism. It is useful and

INTRODUCTION

appropriate to contrast theism and materialism, without simultaneously trying to take up each philosophical or theological variation within each camp. Materialism teaches that all of reality is the sum of matter in motion. For materialists, even those things that are clearly real but not composed of atoms—such as virtues and beauty and love and consciousness—are nonetheless material, in the sense that they exist as an emergent property of matter. Theism, on the other hand, teaches there is something more, something Beyond; an immaterial Presence, and that this implies sentient life beyond organic death. Theism and materialism mark the fault line between fundamentally opposing views of reality.

Invariably critics of theism point to reasons it can't be true, without bothering to explain why materialism is true. Likewise, proponents of theism point to reasons why it must be true, without showing how materialism is false. Both put theism on trial. Seldom is materialism subjected to the same scrutiny. The culture lures us into thinking we can accept or reject theism but not accept or reject the alternative metaphysical position of materialism. One might reject God but grasp only that he's rejected something, not that he's embraced something else. This is a mistake because the relevant choice initially is not among varieties of religious beliefs, but between theist and a-theist metaphysical perspectives. The proposition that matter in motion is all of reality should be proven, just as surely as Christianity, or Islam, or pantheism must be proven. But it can't be, as this book will show.

Most people who are unsettled about the claims of Christianity are not unsettled because they think perhaps God exists but has revealed himself in some other way than is claimed by Christianity. Rather, it is because they have bought into naturalistic Darwinism with all its philosophical ramifications, believing that the only great intellectual exercise is the advance of science, which will someday answer how anything, including but not limited to human beings, exists. Even those untutored in systematic thinking about theology will have some grounding in methodological materialism, because it is necessary to science. We are fundamentally empiricist thinkers, in this society, and we can easily fall into the trap of equating methodological naturalism with philosophical naturalism. Though science is simply not about reality beyond nature, we may come to assume there is no such reality because science doesn't prove it. From this non-sequitur, materialism is given a presumption of validity it shouldn't have.

The better way is to evaluate the evidence available to all of us, from both theist and materialist perspectives. We encounter physical things,

INTRODUCTION

and our understanding about them is enhanced by science. We experience things subjectively, in this body existing in space-time. We are able to consider rationally the phenomena we encounter, and the subjective medium by which we encounter them. This is all evidence. What does it tell us about ultimate reality? Is all of physical reality the result of matter in motion? Or is there necessarily a spiritual reality running in and through that physical reality, and beyond?

The principal theses of this work include the following: (1) The default metaphysical outlook in our culture is materialism; (2) Materialism is an affirmative set of doctrines concerning ultimate reality; (3) Materialism does not adequately explain the evidence available to us; and (4) Theism does.

In the final chapters, we build on what has gone before, saying essentially that if we've established there is some sort of supernatural reality, then it is entirely reasonable to accept the manifestation of God to man in the Christ. In fact, one could fairly conclude that the truth of the Gospel did not merely follow logically from the nature of God as revealed in the arc of history, but that our opportunity for reconciliation with God had to happen the way it did.

Chapter 1: **The Question**

Significance

THERE SEEMS TO BE but two ways of receiving the physical world: as a thing enchanted unto itself, or as a thing just so—a brute fact of physical existence and nothing more. The universe is either alive with meaning and purpose, or it operates mechanistically based on physical laws acting on material things. There is some ultimate significance to how we live this life, or there is nothing beyond physical cause and effect in our actions. Do our lives have significance beyond our daily scrabbling for food, security, acceptance, comfort, and prestige? Is there some ultimate meaning to our being here, or is the intuition of meaning a kind of excess baggage in our biology?

We each of us have a deep intuition of significance. It feels as if there must be some point to our lives, beyond just getting through another day. This intuition is deepened when we consider the alternative of meaninglessness. We are intuitively repulsed by the notion that there is no point to our lives. Or if not repulsed, perhaps sedated, in a manner of speaking, by having pushed the question of meaning outside the periphery of our consciousness. Or we may convince ourselves there is meaning in the very absence of meaning, embracing a kind of existentialist torpor.

This intuition of significance is either an artifact of our biology, merely useful for survival, or it is the recognition of something beyond but also pervading the physical cosmos. There's no middle ground. Either there is no ultimate point to our existence, or there is. If there is, then the source of that meaning has to lie outside ourselves and the physical world we briefly inhabit. And if it lies outside ourselves, that means it lies in a domain conceptually distinct from the world of causes and effects on material things. It is the unseen reality which exists in and through the seen cosmos. It is spiritual reality.

We could call that which is beyond nature *super*-nature, so as to imply that it is beyond nature but also running in and through nature. We might describe an event as being "supernatural," for example, if it in some way defies the laws of physics or is otherwise outside of usual natural processes. That word carries some baggage, however, in that it is sometimes used in the context of ghost stories and the like, which can quickly take us off the point of our inquiry here. So it may better suit our purposes to refer to that which is not physical as being *spiritual*, signifying an animating presence distinct from physical reality, but to which physical reality is in some way subject, so that spiritual reality can rightly be regarded as the superior reality, supervening upon that which is constrained by space and time.

This requires some explanation because of the many ways we use the word "spiritual." We speak of school spirit, or spirit in the sense of being unusually animated, or of distilled "spirits" which alter our thinking. Those are all derivative meanings. The primary meaning of "spirit" is that which stands in opposition to "physical" or "natural." The spiritual realm is understood to be distinct from the physical realm but not spatially or temporally, so it co-exists with us in a way we cannot fully perceive while living in these physical bodies.

This is an inquiry into "metaphysics." Strictly speaking, a naturalist or materialist might be regarded as anti-metaphysical, inasmuch as he believes that that which is physical constitutes all of reality. It would follow that there is no "meta-" physical reality, in that view, and therefore a materialist stands in opposition to any conception of metaphysical reality. The word "metaphysics" is nonetheless sometimes used even by materialists, because it is a useful way to describe things that are admittedly non-physical but nonetheless real, like love or beauty or thought or honor. Materialists might regard those as being emergent properties of that which is physical, rather than being a part of reality distinct from the physical. Their use of "metaphysical" refers to that which is not itself physical, though derived from that which is.

We typically think of supernatural events as intervening or supervening upon natural events. A supernatural cause would intervene if it stopped the natural chain of events and substituted another. We might think of the miracle of virgin birth in this way, for example. Normally, without the joining of human egg and sperm there would be no baby. This is the necessary physical cause of natural conception. An actual virgin birth would have to have a supernatural cause, therefore.

A supernatural cause would supervene if it acted upon natural causes in some way to steer them to a given result. These would presumably be less obvious. If one were to pray for rain and then it rained, for example, there would normally be no way of knowing whether the rain resulted from divine intervention into the physical causes of the rain.

The supernatural is associated with heaven, a "place" that is not really a place in the way we space-bound creatures conceive things. It is understood to be eternal, which we can take to mean characterized by timelessness; that is, existing outside of time rather than in a "place" where time is unending. Thus, there is a realm for a Creator that is outside the creation and from which he creates, such that physical creation is not self-created. That realm is also not limited spatially in the way creation is, because it does not have defining spatial dimensions in the way our physical surroundings do.

The Creator, God, stands outside time and space, except insofar as he chooses to transcend it. In this conception, it would make sense that nature is a subset, so to speak, of super-nature. Heaven suffuses the physical universe, so it is there alongside us all the time, but not apparent to us given our physical limitations.

Supernatural intervention into space and time could manifest physically. This would be a significant proof of the unseen dominion. And so it makes sense that people who are receptive to the idea of this unseen reality would be eagerly on the look-out for such manifestations. It would be easy to be mistaken and assign supernatural significance to merely natural events. But if there is in fact a supernatural reality, and the possibility that it would manifest inside space-time so that it is apparent to us, then people are quite right to look for signs of it.

There has sometimes been an over-eagerness to look for signs of God. When the natural processes around us were less well-understood, there was a tendency to assign to God (or to a god) activity that was actually merely natural. Thunder might be ascribed to the gods' anger, for example. Among Christians there was, in scientifically simpler times, a tendency to God-of-the-gaps thinking, wherein gaps in scientific knowledge were ascribed to mysteries of God. But usually gaps in scientific knowledge mean only that the scientific process has not yet filled in the gap. A gap in knowledge of the natural universe is not by itself proof of God. A God-of-the-gaps mentality is rightly discredited, but that does not mean we should lurch entirely to the opposite error. If there are phenomena unexplained by science, we should not assume a naturalism-of-the-gaps mentality, either.

Instances in which natural processes are suspended or set aside are called miracles. The word "miracle" is sometimes over-used to mean anything that is exciting or complex or heartening or otherwise dear to us, like a child being born or recovery from a grave illness. These may involve supernatural intervention, but may not, and the immediate causes are usually explainable by reference to natural processes. As miraculous as new parents might regard the arrival of a new baby, there is a biological explanation for it.

There is a sense, however, in which even such events as recovery from illness or birth of a baby might be regarded as having supernatural origin, though such origin might be so attenuated that "miraculous" is not the right word for it. It is proposed, by many religious belief systems, that there is some sense in which God, who presides over this natural realm, has a continuing involvement with it. Not only in the sense of intervening in ways large and small, from time to time, but also in the sense of a continuing, supervening, upholding of the world. If there is a supernatural reality that is far beyond the limitations of our presently space- and time-bound existence, it is not far-fetched that there is some constant infusion of God-stuff, for want of a better word, that maintains the world as we know it. That God-stuff might be called love, or common grace.

Theism vs. Materialism

If there is a spiritual reality which imparts meaning to humanity, then there must be God. We can conceive of God as the First Cause, and the ultimate superlative to which all human-understood ideals point. It would take this omnipotent source of Being-in-itself to impart genuine meaning or purpose to humanity. A being less than all-powerful and all-good God would yield a counterfeit sense of purpose.

But perhaps this intuition of significance is an illusion. We readily suppose there is a spiritual reality, but we can un-imagine it. We can attempt to conceive of the cosmos as reducible to matter in motion, and nothing more. Immensely complex, but not enlivened by anything beyond it. We can imagine there is no master intelligence, in the universe, and that the intelligence of human beings derives from matter, not the ultimate Mind of God. Matter, in this imagining, creates mind, not the other way around.

The question is whether the evidence points to God, or is better explained by materialism. Materialism (or naturalism) is the spirit of the age, following an epoch of specifically Christian theism, which followed an epoch of paganism. In our culture, when a person rejects God, he doesn't typically adopt paganism or pantheism instead. Usually the turn is, perhaps unwittingly, to materialism.

Every person who ever considers questions of ultimate reality has to work from the evidence available. Intuition of significance is a form of evidence, and so are physical things accessible to our senses. And so is the rationality of the human mind, and the universal moral sense, and the marvelous order of the cosmos. These and other bits of evidence can be evaluated on the basis of theism, and of materialism, and that's what is undertaken in this book. "Theism" is the belief that God is, and that he is active in the world. "Materialism" is the belief that there is no God, therefore all evidence must be explained in terms of matter and physical forces acting on it. These two visions of reality are mutually exclusive.

Definitions

Among the difficulties of perceiving the metaphysical viewpoint in opposition to theism is that of simple labeling. What word do we attach? "Materialism" is used here, but it can easily be confused with another definition the word carries: acting upon acquisitiveness, greed, avarice, or the tendency to identify with one's consumer choices. In philosophical terms, however, "materialism" refers to matter, the physical stuff of the universe. Matter is subject to physical forces, so we can refer to materialism as matter-in-motion, an irreducible description of the physical stuff of the cosmos.

"Naturalism" refers to belief solely in nature, which in turn refers to the physical universe, as distinct from any spiritual reality which may or may not run in and through physical things. So "naturalism" would also be a serviceable label for the metaphysical worldview principally in opposition to theism, in the modern age. But this label, too, is potentially confusing. "Nature" is also used to refer to plants and animals and their interactions in ecosystems of the earth. Or to distinguish environments that are relatively untouched by mankind, like old-growth woodlands or uncultivated prairies or ocean deeps. "Nature" by that definition distinguishes between mankind and its influences, on the one hand, and the rest of the living world, on the other. A person who studies nature so described, or simply has a strong affinity for it, might be called a "naturalist." "Nature" and "naturalism" are not used in this book to refer to nature-lover endeavors, however, but rather in a philosophical sense, essentially a synonym for materialism. Naturalism describes the belief system which holds that everything is explainable by natural processes;

that all of reality consists of matter and forces acting on it according to physical laws; that there is no God and no supernatural reality of any kind. Theism and naturalism stand in fundamental opposition.

While we're making important word distinctions, let's consider the word "reality." We sometimes speak loosely of reality when we mean only the physical cosmos, but that is a mistake if there is also a spiritual realm standing behind and through it. If there's something other than nature, then reality encompasses that, too. Reality is the largest conceptual net one can cast. It's important, when speaking of reality, not to assume away the existence of unseen spiritual reality.

Enchantment

The difference between these two competing worldviews—theism and materialism—is profound. Which is true? This is the most important question for any individual, and for any society. We may live with an upward call from the prosaic claims of the body to the poetry of the soul in communion with God. Or we may live with a human-centered downcast view, in which ideals are merely phenomena emergent from operation of myriad natural causes and effects.

The philosopher Max Weber, borrowing conceptually from Friedrich Schiller, wrote near the end of the nineteenth century of his concern about the effects of the "disenchantment" of the world. In traditional society imbued with religious belief, he wrote, "the world remains a great enchanted garden,"* because there is an unseen supernatural reality not fully knowable in this life, and which may impact the natural world in unpredictable ways. It lends an uplifting aura of significance to human agency. Religion is rationalized away, however, in the modern, "enlightened" empiricist age, taking with it the sense of magic animating the physical world. Whether the object of religious belief is true was not the immediate point, for Weber and others who thought like him. His concern was with the impact disenchantment has on a society which rationalizes it away. Matthew Arnold wrote on this eloquently at mid-nineteenth century, in his famous poem *Dover Beach*.

A more recent philosopher, Charles Taylor, was concerned for what he called the loss of the "imaginary," by which he meant not the loss of something fictional, but the loss of something mentally "imaged;" accessible only

---

*Weber, Sociology of Religion (1922); English translation (of fourth edition) by Ephraim Fischoff 1963.

to the mind. A theist would include in this definition faith, which Hebrews 11:1 tells us is "the assurance of things hoped for, the conviction of things not seen." The existence of the unseen world is rejected, by naturalism. Many people, including people with faith and some without faith, believe this disenchantment leaves us intellectually and spiritually impoverished.

The loss of enchantment is a subject of remark by poets and thinkers not just because they're looking at changes in themselves, or in changes occurring society-wide only within their lifetime. They're looking at a longer progression than that, a historical trend measured in lifetimes. How an individual perceives the world—with or without some measure of enchantment—is influenced more by the era in which he lives, than the circumstances of his own life. We are a social people, with a shared cultural memory. The beliefs we individually adopt—in particular the two competing worldviews discussed here—are very much influenced by those of people around us. It's not purely a matter of rational argument and debate. In consequence, this central issue of our existence is in play collectively and intergenerationally.

The concern is whether as a society our over-all thriving is keeping up with our material prosperity. Could the disenchantment of the world be behind increased reports of depression, loneliness, civil strife, disintegration of families, crime, hopelessness, drug abuse, suicide? If people internalize a materialist view of reality, they are necessarily internalizing certain of its necessary corollaries, like meaninglessness. On the other hand, the truth is truth. We don't adopt beliefs because they're helpful. We should believe or disbelieve on the sole criterion of truth.

Evidence

Why does anyone ever believe anything? The self reaches out through the intentionality of consciousness to evaluate evidence. That evidence can take many forms. Some more direct; some more reliable; and all interpreted subjectively. It can be confusing and may seem conflicting. The difficulty is in applying the correct ordering criteria in our thinking. Not every thought or observation is equally helpful. What we should be about is a methodology of discovering truth that is comprehensive and reasonable.

"Evidence" is a word often confused with argument, such as when one means, by "evidence," only that which supports his point of view. That sort of exclusion of evidence games the debate. Atheists sometimes say for example that faith is belief not supported by evidence, but that's not so. Evidence takes many forms, starting with simple observation but including our reason, as well. Observation refers to reception of data through the sense of sight. Reception of data through the senses is an empirical undertaking, and is the foundation of science. Empirical observation does not require the philosophy of *empiricism*, however; the theory that all knowledge results only from sense experience. In this age we place so much emphasis on the accomplishments of science that it has become commonplace to think of science as the sole source of knowledge, and empiricism as the sole basis of science. Because science is the study of material things, materialism as an explanation for all of reality seems to follow. But it doesn't. It's certainly true that we know things because of the systematic observations of science, but observation itself is possible only because of features of human consciousness not explainable by science, but explainable by spiritual reality. Necessary features of the physical cosmos we observe are explainable only if there is a spiritual reality beyond it.

In addition to this potential confusion about what constitutes evidence, sometimes polemic ends are served by calling "evidence" that which is mere argument, for example when artificial filters are imposed so that valid evidence is excluded for spurious reasons. Or evidence may be filtered out by vaguely defining word meanings, so the hearer naturally attaching one meaning is then led subtly to substitute another, thus eclipsing the original meaning.

Another way of distorting evidence is to impose inappropriate burdens of proof. The effect of imposing a burden of proof is to establish a presumption of correctness by default. If you're a religion skeptic, you may expect God to be proven to you, and proven to a high level of certainty. But why? Why would theism have to be proven, and not materialism? If you're a theist puzzled by atheism, you might similarly be tempted to say materialism bears a burden of proof that theism does not.

Here's an example of an improper burden of proof. Carl Sagan asserted that "extraordinary claims require extraordinary evidence," and this aphorism has been often repeated to promote skepticism of the claim that God is. It seems innocuous enough, superficially, but what it does is establish a presumption of correctness where it doesn't belong. The God proposition is extraordinary only if an orthodoxy of materialism is presumed correct. One could as well apply the standard to the materialist hypothesis. Based on current science of origins, materialism would suppose that all matter is self-created *ex nihilio*. Isn't that a rather more extraordinary claim?

The point can be illustrated by contrasting the theism vs. materialism debate to a criminal trial. In a criminal trial, we deliberately establish a burden of proof. The government must prove guilt; the defense does not have to prove innocence. We make innocence the default; the presumptively correct position. We purposely impose this burden on one side, the prosecution, because the truth-seeking process is fallible, and we prefer wrongful acquittals to wrongful convictions. We know that a guilty person may go free, and, much more seriously, an innocent person may be convicted. Those possibilities are known on the front end, and are factored into how the trial is conducted, so that guilt, not innocence, must be proven. The burden of proof is valid, in criminal cases.

But not on the question whether there is a God. There is no reason to build in a preference for materialism; in fact doing so interferes with the search for truth. The approach ought to be to evaluate the evidence in light of the opposing worldviews of materialism and theism. And then, follow that evidence wherever it leads, on this most important of questions.

Chapter 2: **Intuition**

WE HAVE ALL FELT an inarticulable leaning one way or the other on a particular subject. We have all felt a vague sense of apprehension or excitement or dread, without being able to say specifically why. It is possible to pause and apply our rational faculties to that feeling, to consider whether there is some external evidence we might have overlooked. Oftentimes there is not. We just "sense" things, though it is not really through the senses that the thing is perceived.

Are there intuitions that inhere in our intellectual and emotional make-up, and are they reliable? Do we have any hard-wiring, so to speak, which precedes our acquisition of information? Are we born as a blank slate, or is there a self in place when learning commences? Does our development depend entirely on nurture, or is there a mental content we are born with, naturally and materially?

Have you ever felt a sense of astonishment? I don't mean being startled or surprised. I mean astonished: a feeling of awe and wonder, perhaps from seeing something in a fresh light, which shakes us from the mundane. Sometimes we feel this way when introduced to a newborn baby, for example. We remember again, because we forget during the course of a normal day, how astonishing it is that we have life at all. We can appreciate vicariously the sense of wonder a child has, seeing things anew through the child's eyes.

The idea that there is a special receptivity in children is not new. Here is a portion of William Wordsworth's poem (mid-nineteenth century) *Intimations of Immortality From Recollections of Early Childhood*:

> There was a time when meadow, grove, and stream,
> The earth, and every common sight,
> To me did seem
> Apparelled in celestial light,
> The glory and the freshness of a dream.

CHAPTER 2: INTUITION

* * *

—But there's a Tree, of many, one,
A single Field which I have looked upon,
Both of them speak of something that is gone:
The Pansy at my feet
Doth the same tale repeat:
Whither is fled the visionary gleam?
Where is it now, the glory and the dream?

He acknowledges a child's "visionary gleam," but also laments its loss. The world seems enchanted, to children, and we lose some of that sense of enchantment as we grow into skeptical adulthood. But what if the sense of enchantment, more pronounced in childhood, is valid evidence on its own of "celestial light" in the world?

At around the turn of the last century a theologian named Rudolf Otto tried to articulate a feeling of aliveness and of sensitivity that is not rooted in the self, or in the senses, or in our reasoning. He described what we perceive in this way, spiritually, as "numinous;" something outside ourselves, that we experience as an energy or presence or aura around other living things. Because the thing we perceive is not visual, it is not perfectly accurate to describe this phenomenon as numinous "light," but this is the closest analogy we have, using the language of the senses. So "numinous light" refers to that felt sense of the presence of divinity, that we all have but may lose if it is not recognized and cultivated.

This numinous light of childhood is a sense of enchantment that fades as the child grows older. That perception of the numinous exists as an intuition, in children, before it is suppressed or squeezed out of us by the hard realities of life. The point is, that it's a real thing, if difficult to describe. And it came into being with the child, the child didn't learn it. The child was born with a sense of astonishment. Adults have similar moments of astonishment, especially if we cultivate it by trying to see things in a fresh way. That openness to a feeling of astonishment at what we encounter in the world might be instinctive. It might be one of the few things that we come into the world with, so that we're not born as computers with the operating system in place but no real content until life works on us and supplies it.

The presence or absence of intuitions has important epistemological implications. If we are born with true intuition, that means we come into the world with, at a minimum, some sort of informational content. This is at a moment when it cannot be said that our thinking is in any way corrupted by the world. If we are not born with any intuition concerning reality, then we are truly blank slates at birth. Our awareness of the marvelous and sometimes malevolent complexity of the world around us would all have developed *ab initio* inside the operating system and memory of the brain.

There has long been a postulate among some philosophers that we have an intuition of God's existence. This intuition, it is believed, is a *sensus divinatus*, a felt sense of God's presence. Many highly-regarded thinkers, like Augustine, Calvin, and (a contemporary) Alvin Plantinga, regard this intuition as basic in epistemology; meaning, that it is as fundamentally a basis for knowing as is rational thought based on external evidence. Not only is this intuition reliable unto itself, but according to Plantinga it means we can attach meaning to the sense of yearning we all feel for that which we can but dimly perceive. That yearning points us to something higher, to a possible fulfillment of that yearning in God's love.

In the materialist view of reality, intuitions are either denied or explained as evolved phenomena only. If we sense God's presence, it could be learned rather than intuitive, as a result of motivators like fear of the unknown or a desire to have some control, through appeal to divine agency, over the scary and seemingly random things that happen. These would derive from our biology. Indeed, we could be born with the intuition of God even if there were no God. We would have an operating system which includes a receptivity to supernatural explanations because response to fear enhances survival. But in this instance biological evolution would have generated a false signal: intuition of a non-existent element of reality. The simpler explanation for the intuition is that it points to something real.

It's astonishing that anything exists at all. There's no discernible reason for it. And yet we don't walk around with a sense of astonishment in every waking minute. We are inured to the fact of things as they are. We are habituated against regarding them as if for the first time. We can recover that sense of astonishment, however, and it is worthwhile to try to do so because existence of material things really is astonishing, if we consider that there's no particular reason it had to be thus. There could be nothing, and no you to be reading this. But there is something, and you are you. Why?

There is a background buzz in every mind, unless self-created noise drowns it out. A big "Why" that disturbs or ought to. We live with a primordial agitation of mind (in David Bentley Hart's phrasing*) moving us to ask: *how and why am I here?* We put these kinds of questions in a basket

---

*The Experience of God: Being, Consciousness, Bliss (2014).

marked "ineffable;" also the mind's venue for God. The fact of material existence ought to belong in that same category. We should recover our intuition that the existence of anything at all is utterly astonishing.

Do you remember the first time you saw the ocean? Did you feel a sense of astonishment then? You must have, if you saw it as a child, or saw it first as an adult and managed not to file the data away as merely one more naturally occurring and pleasing phenomenon. There ought to be a catch in the imagination at that sight; or, similarly, at the sight of endless sand dunes, or majestic mountains, or brilliant sunsets. Their beauty points us again to the marvel that things exist at all. If we achieve that sense of wonder at physical existence, then even mundane things become astonishing, though there aren't additional reasons like beauty to make them so. And then we may realize that the existence of the cosmos and of the world, not to mention human beings in it, is so surprising and unnecessary that it points to a distinct spiritual reality beyond.

Chapter 3: **Existence of Physical Things**

"Nothing"

IMAGINE TRUE NOTHINGNESS. It's not easy to do, because the very act of contemplating "nothing" seems to make it a something. We have to imagine no physical forces acting on matter, and we have to imagine no matter at all. No light. No thought. No potentiality of any kind, either, which might actualize into an atom, a rational inference, or a spiritual presence, "hovering over the face of the waters" or otherwise. Nothingness would not merely be material that is well-spaced or which seems mostly unaffected by distant physical forces. Instead: nothing. No mind of man or God to think of the nothing. No rock, no speck of dust, no dark matter, no gravity, no space. "What rocks dream about," Aristotle supposedly said.

We find it difficult to conceptualize true nothingness because we exist in space and time, and true nothingness would negate those physical dimensions. When we contemplate true nothingness we do so with space- and time-bound brains, trying to conceptualize an entire absence of space- and time-bound things, including brains. Like spirit, nothingness is a metaphysical concept. Conceptualizing true nothingness requires holding in the physical mind that which is beyond physical, in the same way that conceptualizing the spiritual requires holding in the physical mind that which is beyond physical.

To grasp the significance of true nothing, consider that it is categorically like both materialism and theism. It constitutes a distinct paradigm of reality, in contrast to the paradigm in which reality is composed only of material things and forces, and the paradigm in which reality includes a spiritual realm actively supervening upon the material. There are but three available paradigms of reality. One is nothingness. Two is materialism. Three is spiritual running through and beyond material. These paradigms are necessarily mutually exclusive, because each is a picture of all of reality. One of these three must be true; the other two must be false.

CHAPTER 3: EXISTENCE OF PHYSICAL THINGS

The current science of origins tells us there was true nothing, and then there was the something of physical things. This is a complete shift from one version of reality, to another irreconcilable version of reality. We would have to imagine this occurred with no divine agency involved, if there is no God. This theorized absence of intervening agency would seem to invalidate both true nothingness and materialism as adequate explanations of reality. That leaves a reality which includes spirit. Theism holds there was never a true nothing, because in the beginning there was already God, and God was the agency which brought forth the physical something from the void.

If we can grasp the concept of true nothingness, then we can grasp the concept of spiritual reality. Against a backdrop of true nothingness, the existence of the somethingness of the cosmos truly is astonishing, and it cannot explain its own existence.

First Cause

If we are to imagine natural causes for everything, as science does, then the existence of things as they are right now is explained by the existence of things as they were a moment ago, subjected to natural processes acting on things in the expected way. In this limited, moment-by-moment way of thinking about existence, the present state of the universe is perhaps not so astonishing. It's the state of the universe a moment ago, with continued physical causes acting on matter, resulting in the state of the universe right now.

Of course, that's not at all what we mean when we ponder the ultimate origin of existing things. If we were satisfied with the explanation that this moving car exists in this spot at this moment because it existed in that spot the moment before, then existence would be no mystery at all. But of course we're not satisfied with that. Every instance of causation begs the question what causes preceded that cause, and the cause before, and so on back to the first cause. The study of physical causation is integral to science, but the question of ultimate physical causation—the first uncaused-cause—is necessarily one of philosophy. Science is the study of physical things, but the first cause of physical things preceded physical things. So the question of the first cause stands apart from science. It is a question of philosophy, or theology.

A person can in theory extrapolate his physical existence in this moment, with all his physical attributes at this moment, backward through all his physical states in all the moments leading up to this one. Each moment and each development depends on what came before. Using the language of the philosophy of causation, we could say we are each "contingent" beings, meaning that our current existence is contingent upon prior states of existence. Most of what we experience physically is contingently caused, meaning that those experiences are not self-caused. Existence at moment #2 is contingent upon existence at moment #1.

A person can trace his bodily existence to his parents' contributions of DNA, and the existence of his parents to their parents', and so on, all the way back to the first persons. If people evolved from other life forms, then that tracing-back would go back through those predecessor beings all the way back to first life. That first life would be traced to non-living materials, and those materials to prior aggregations of material. All of these beings and things in the chain of causation of a human body exist contingently. They are not self-caused.

The same would be true for physical things other than human beings. If we could trace back all the extremely large but finite number of causes, and causes of causes, the chain of causation would not extend backward into infinity. The chain must begin at a point that is not contingently caused, but is instead the first cause of all subsequent causes.

The question how there could be physical things at all has long been a matter of philosophical conjecture. Aristotle, for example, considered the contingent nature of physical things, acknowledging the chain of physical causation going back to a first uncaused-cause. He did so employing the concept of *teleology*—purposefulness in things over time. Existence is linked to motion. Everything that moves, moves as a result of prior motion. But what about the first motion? There had to be a "Prime Mover," equivalent to the "uncaused cause." These relate to the idea of contingency: all is potential until it is actualized, and nothing potential can actualize itself. The prime mover; the uncaused cause, is pure actuality, and we assign to that pure actuality the description "God." There's much more to this, in philosophical refinements to Aristotle's thought, but the central idea is that physical things are not self-created; there had to be a Creator of them. Every material thing in the cosmos relies upon some immaterial "thing" outside of it. Even if we were to conclude that God never intervenes in that natural reality (that is, no miracles, no Incarnation, and no Resurrection), there still had to be an outside agency to light the fuse for the Big Bang.

CHAPTER 3: EXISTENCE OF PHYSICAL THINGS

Something from Nothing

The Big Bang is the current best scientific explanation for the origin of the physical universe. The idea is that all physical things emerged from nothing, in the sudden expansion of extremely dense matter, continuing to expand outward into the entire physical content of the universe. This is extrapolated through the movement of all physical things, developing into the universe recognizable to us at this moment. We think of "empty" outer space as nothing, but it's actually something. It's full of material with physical forces acting upon it. If we turn from super-large things, like galaxies, to super-small things, like the "space" inside a molecule, we still cannot call that space "nothing," because galaxies and particles act as they do because of physical forces. Physical things large and small move, and that movement is caused by physical forces: gravity, electromagnetism, and the small and weak nuclear forces. It is theorized there was nothing and then there was something, physical things with natural forces acting on them, expanding rapidly to constitute the universe we now know. Something, in other words, comes from nothing.

Perhaps the Big Bang is the correct explanation for the current state of the universe, but it doesn't explain how the Something of the universe in its first moments came into being from the Nothing that immediately preceded it. The theory holds that time, too, originated with the Big Bang, so it really makes no sense to think in terms of the "moment" before the Big Bang. It is conceived to be a spontaneous generation of all the material that would become the universe. The Something-from-Nothing problem is unanswerable by materialism. Physical things can come from other physical things, but not from true nothing. Nothing cannot *cause* something, either, whether it be the Big Bang or time or consciousness or the tiniest subatomic particle in existence. So the expectation should be that something outside the system of physical things (like God) created the physical things, bringing them into being. Perhaps by means of a Big Bang. The fact of there being any physical thing whatsoever argues for theism. If there was nothing, and then something, some non-physical agency had to pre-exist the something.

While we do science by assuming there are natural explanations for the phenomena we encounter, the assumption is not valid everywhere and at all times. There are deviations from natural explanation, as with miracles, and as with ultimate origins. They are so significantly exceptional that we can move forward with the scientific project employing methodological naturalism, but we have to be cautious not to slip into thinking that naturalism is synonymous with science.

In fact, we'd do well to remember that science is made possible by the predictability of physical things; its orderliness. That orderliness does not explain itself, either. When we think of the origins of physical things, we tend to think of rocks hurtling through space; three-dimensional objects of various kinds. But physical reality is not just material composed of compounds of elements and atoms and subatomic particles. Physical reality also includes the forces acting on that material, so that movement and change occur within the additional dimension of time. This adds energy to the mix. The origins of these features are not themselves explained naturally.

There are activists for the materialist philosophical position, however, who nonetheless attempt to defend it as against this difficulty. For example, in 2012 physicist Lawrence Krauss attempted an explanation, in his book *A Universe From Nothing,* but this turned out to be an explanation of something-from-something-else. Physicists who undertake the task of bringing questions of philosophy into their science sometimes make category mistakes, such as inadvertently tweaking the word "nothing" to mean something other than nothing. Philosophers can contemplate the something-from-nothing proposition though science can't. Or to say it differently, when we study physical material and forces, we're doing science; when we consider questions like how something can come from nothing, we're doing philosophy. Science does not prove the presence or absence of reality apart from that which is the study of science: the physical cosmos only.

Chapter 4: **Nature**

Causation

IN THE LAST CHAPTER we considered the fact of physical existence. In this chapter we consider certain features of it, beginning with *causation*. Not the ultimate causation of the philosophically necessary uncaused-cause, but rather ordinary causation as the central concept in natural processes, which, according to materialism, is all there is.

Natural events are the norm in our everyday experience. Natural events are those which are traceable directly to other natural events. Rain, for example, is commonly caused by condensation of water vapor in the air, which is in turn caused by evaporation of surface water. That's not to say there could not be a supernatural cause directly, or a supernatural intervention into prior natural causes, but events like rain are natural. They are orderly and amenable to scientific study. Most of what happens that we can observe happens naturally; as the result of natural processes which we can see, and study, and understand. Why we would say one thing *causes* another is actually a more complicated philosophical question than one might think; perhaps nowhere more so than with respect to our thought-life: how one thought "causes" another. For ordinary physical events, however, we can usually, with the aid of science, figure out an event's causes, and the causes of those causes, and so on. Sometimes we can't, and science moves forward on those frontiers. But it's noteworthy that in pursuing causes scientifically, we assume there *is* a natural cause, and that it is discoverable. We do that because we understand the world to have order; that there are natural explanations for most events; which is another way of saying there are natural *causes* for most events.

Causation is a function of time. Time is more limited and more limiting than we imagine it to be. Time constrains our experience of being much like the three spatial dimensions do. Time doesn't peel off in increments, it is a fluid thing, but let's imagine we can nonetheless capture the state of things moment by moment. Physical things exist in three dimensions of space: length, width, and height. If there were no dimension of time, the universe would be static. It would be interesting to stand outside of it and take our time studying it, but we can't "take our time" if there's no time. We'd be frozen in that static moment, too, with not even a thought in play. But of course the universe is not static, it is constantly changing, and that change is a function of time. It is also a function of physical forces acting on physical things, resulting in changed physical states. An asteroid hits the moon and causes material to shift, resulting in a crater. The movement of a butterfly wing contributes, ever so imperceptibly, to the movement of air.

A planet or subatomic particle occupies one physical position at one moment, and another physical position at the next moment. The position of all the planets and particles at one moment is acted on by physical forces so that those physical things occupy another position in the next moment. We routinely think in terms of force acting on matter on an axis of time as constituting physical causation, but why? We've skipped a step, really, when we do that. What is the nature of the connection between the first event which we say "causes" the second, and so on? We see smoke rise from a fire, and regard that as "natural," but why, really? Is it strictly a function of time; i.e. event #2 follows sequentially event #1? And does so consistently? We observe properties of fire and of smoke and of atmosphere and believe we've explained this instance of causation, but we haven't fully explained the physical phenomenon of causation in the abstract.

Nonetheless, we look about us and see that the physical state of the universe now existing appears to be the result of the state of the universe the moment before. Natural processes are in play throughout the universe all the time. The state of the universe a moment ago is the sum of all those natural processes before that moment. The state of the universe now is the sum of the natural continued movement in all those natural processes, from the preceding moment to now. The physical processes of the universe a moment ago in that sense *caused* the universe now. We can reasonably assume for purposes of doing science (and materialists will insist for all purposes) that the state of the universe at this moment is dictated by the state of the universe in the preceding moment.

The state of the universe at any one moment is comprised of such an unimaginably large number of variables that it is tempting to say they are "infinite." But it's important to note that the number, though large quite beyond our ability to reckon, is necessarily finite. This is an important point

CHAPTER 4: NATURE

to understand because if we are to make sense of existing things materially, based on causation, we can't add unknown variables to the mix willy-nilly. If we imagine the causes to be infinite, the universe would be inexplicable, and science would be impossible. We understand (and our understanding is ever expanding) that most of what we encounter physically has a natural explanation, which means it derives from natural causes. That means the chains of causation could theoretically be traced backward along those natural causes to a point of beginning. There are certainly an extremely large number of physical causes, and they are complexly interrelated, and we could never hope to identify them all, but they are necessarily finite in number.

An implication of this finitude is *determinism*. If there are a finite number of physical causes for the state of the universe at this moment, and if there are no supernatural inputs, then once the universe is in existence, it must necessarily change over time in one and only one way. This is what we mean when we say the state of the universe at one moment *determines* the state of the universe at the next. It is the same as saying the universe at the present moment was *caused by* the state of the universe in the moment preceding. If we imagine that the universe suddenly sprang into existence from nothing in one moment (as with the Big Bang theory of origins), then, if there are no supernatural inputs into the natural processes thereafter, the subsequent states of the universe are necessarily determined at the moment of the Big Bang.

So as not to veer too far from our consideration of the character of physical things, let's put to one side this idea of determinism, for the nonce. For now we can merely note that an element of the materialist worldview is that things must unfold in the one and only manner; that which the unimaginably large but finite number of material vectors dictates. This has profound implications for our ideas of personal autonomy, agency, and moral freedom.

We can explain much of natural causation through science, but at least three things concerning causation we cannot: the First Cause, discussed in the preceding chapter; the consistency with which material is formed and by which natural forces act on material, discussed in the next chapter; and the provenance of the phenomenon of physical causation in the abstract.

Origin of Life

How did life originate? This is a very different question from that of the origin of all physical existence. It is a special case of origin. In the first seconds and minutes and years and millenia of the universe, there were no people or algae or single-celled organisms. Living things came much later. Either they were created by God, or they came into being by *abiogenesis*. Abiogenesis is the materialist explanation for the origin of living things. It is the theory that inorganic matter developed into increasingly complex organic compounds, which in turn developed characteristics we associate with life. Much thought has been poured into how this might have occurred, because it is immensely important to the ideology of materialism. The materialist perspective excludes the possibility of any kind of outside God-like agency, therefore life must be explained from the ground-up, so to speak; as a self-created thing. Because naturalism supposes there is no Creator, it seeks to explain life some other way. Much speculation is given, therefore, to how first life might have formed from non-life. Efforts to recreate abiogenesis have been unsuccessful. There was for a time at mid-twentieth century some headway in formation of simple amino acids, but it ended there, with some material we would call organic, but not living. The effort proceeds on theories that life began in extreme conditions no longer present on earth, or not easily accessible.

It is important to distinguish between the questions of life's origins and life's development. Biological development is most usually explained by naturalistic evolution, among those who subscribe to naturalism, and among many theists, as well. Materialists typically believe that non-teleological Darwinian evolution is a complete and sufficient explanation for all biological development. It doesn't explain the first instance of life, however. A materialist would have to admit to not knowing how life began, even if he buys wholesale into naturalistic Darwinian evolution.

Life in its currently complex forms is the result of purely natural processes, according to naturalistic evolution. The theory supposes this to be true going backward to simpler and simpler life forms, all the way back to the most primitive organisms. The theory of evolution thus seductively leads us to think backward in time with an assumption that whatever the explanation for first life was, it must have been of solely natural origin. Perhaps with electricity in a watery place with just the right combination of chemical compounds to form amino acid chains and then lipids which structurally enclose cell structures which encourage more complex amino acids, and so on.

This is interesting speculation, but naturalistic Darwinian evolution does not by itself support the inference that the first instances of life occurred naturally. Evolution is about development of life once it exists, not about its origin. There is no reason to suppose that first life emerged through natural mechanisms, rather than being created by an external Creator, even if naturalistic evolution were the explanation for all life developing thereafter.

Moreover, even if first life came about in thermal vents or in some primordial soup, this would mean only that natural processes were at work even at these earliest of stages in the formation of life. If there is a God, it was he who created the natural processes. If life came about from the germ of non-living material, that would not preclude God's creation of life, through natural processes acting on material that he also created.

Evolution

Of course, the evidence includes a diversity and complexity of life far beyond the simplest of organic compounds. To get from simple amino acids to something as complicated as a human being through a process of naturalistic evolution, we have to imagine variation within a population of a kind of living thing, and the population subjected to environmental pressure, with the result that some combinations of genetic variants survive, and others die. That results in a different mix of variables in the population, and the process repeats.

Though this is referred to as "adaptation" or "natural selection," these phrases are potentially misleading. There is no adapting or selecting going on. Neither individuals nor populations purpose to adapt. The survival conditions do no selecting. It is entirely a passive process, so no active-voice description really fits. Instead, conditions in populations and environment change with the result that populations are better fitted to their physical circumstances. Minute incremental changes over time are said to result in greater fitness of the population for survival in its environment, and this process extends even to speciation and divisions of phyla.

Usually, when evolution is discussed, naturalistic evolution is assumed. But evolution does not necessitate naturalism. To understand this, let's again consider *teleology*. Teleology means purpose or design in nature. Materialism precludes teleology. Materialism requires an absence of purpose or design, as is clear from a proper understanding of naturalistic evolution. No external driver is imagined for the process. Living things result from passive deselection of traits in prior populations as a result of environment. If we imagine there is some external driver for the process (most obviously, God) then we abandon naturalistic evolution, and adopt teleological evolution.

Aristotle adopted the concept of design or purpose in nature in his analysis of causation, as explaining the "why" of matter in addition to efficient physical causes. The combination of causes point to a purposefulness of physical change. The word (again: "teleology") is used more generally to refer to purposefulness in the abstract, which in turn implies design in physical things. Teleology inheres in some theisms. If there is a God who designed the universe and created it and directs its progress for his purposes, then we can say history itself is teleological.

Biological evolution is, according to the theory, a natural process. That does not require the conclusion that it is entirely unguided by God, however. Most of what we observe in nature consists of natural processes, as we have noted. That's what makes science possible. But the fact of natural processes does not exclude the intervention of supernatural input. There are some fairly significant problems with evolution theory that are difficult to overcome if there is not, at some point and in some fashion, a Designer's intervention to propel biological development forward.

The point is that there is a distinction between naturalistic evolution and teleological evolution. Naturalistic evolution is frequently assumed in discussions of evolution. Teleological evolution supposes that a Creator employs natural processes to advance the development of life into greater diversity and complexity. Materialism is so well ingrained in scientific discussions of evolution that people often overlook the problems with it, both as philosophy and as a complete explanation of biological development. If there is a gap in understanding, we're expected to assume that science will eventually fill it consistently with the philosophy of materialism.

Evolution, in its naturalistic form, is often invoked as an intellectual wedge. It is thought to set religion and science in opposition each to the other. It sets up a divide between, on the one hand, what is considered fact-driven, rational, evidence-based atheistic naturalism; and on the other hand, emotion-driven, irrational, evidence-free religious faith. This is a false dualism. The philosophy of naturalism is actually accepted on faith,

CHAPTER 4: NATURE

smuggled in through a distortion of what science is. Science is by definition only the study of material things; it does not address reality beyond material things or phenomena said to emerge from them. It certainly does not disprove a spiritual reality.

Non-teleological evolution is sometimes described as "Darwin's dangerous idea," because it is thought to dispense with the need for a Creator altogether. Of course it does not speak to first life or first material existence or first information or first causes, as well as having some serious explanatory gaps. Still, because it is presented as such a thoroughgoing explanation of biological development, it can seem no supernatural component is needed. "Darwinism" has come to mean not simply evolution, but naturalistic evolution; and not simply naturalistic evolution, but a bottom-up view of everything, dispensing with God altogether. The idea is that if life can develop purely naturally from the simplest organic compounds to mankind, then all other complexities of the physical world can similarly be considered bottom-up developments, rather than top-down creations. Instead of imagining an omnipotent God who draws physical reality up to himself from the simplest base materials (like Adam formed from dust), we are to imagine nothingness becoming something and then something becoming simple living things, and then development of living things to greater and greater complexity, including human beings who then invent God. If we are to adopt a bottom-up orientation as Darwinian naturalistic evolution seems to suggest, then we dethrone God and substitute ourselves as the pinnacle of natural "creation." On this view, we create God, rather than the other way around, and God exists only in our shared cultural memory to orient our thinking for reasons of evolutionary success rather than truth.

Non-teleological biological evolution describes a natural process. There are many such natural processes at work all around us, all the time. As I write, a hurricane is headed toward the east coast of the United States. That is a natural process, too. To be sure, there are many, many variables in play, involving prevailing winds, temperature gradients in the atmosphere and in the water, the rotation of the earth, and many others. Not an infinite number of variables, mind, but a number large enough to almost seem that way to us. If it were possible to know all the variables, it would be possible to know exactly where and when the hurricane would make landfall, and to what effect. That's because the hurricane is a natural process. Absent divine intervention, it will play out just as the combination of physical variables requires. This is a movement of matter in the physical world. Absent divine intervention; that is, the mind of God, it is purely a physical process.

Physical processes include not just weather, but the movement of bodies in space, and tectonic movements, and much human activity, including conception, fetal development, and birth. There may be divine (supernatural) intervention in part, in these processes, in ways we don't see, but generally we count on natural processes being entirely natural processes. That's what enables us to do science, which is by definition the study of only natural processes. Indeed, the regularity of natural processes is what enables us to identify miracles as being such, because they are rare deviations. Jesus performed miracles to show supernatural intervention resulting in *exceptions* to natural processes. Joseph assumed (wrongly, as it turned out) Mary's infidelity, because he knew where babies come from *naturally*. It has never been the case that people looked around in uncomprehending wonder to imagine spiritual drivers for everything that happens.

Natural and supernatural processes are not mutually exclusive. The existence of natural processes does not negate the possibility of supernatural intervention. This would be true for the natural process of biological evolution, if it were to turn out to be a correct explanation for the development of life. Biological evolution would not rule out supernatural truth any more than would hurricanes. Nor would it require a conclusion that all features of a human being, including his consciousness, are the result of a natural process of biological evolution. If the human brain evolved, it does not necessarily follow that human consciousness merely emerges as a property of that physical brain.

Chapter 5: **Ideals**

WE'RE CONSIDERING THE FACT of physical existence by considering how existing things are caused. For the reasons we've covered, physical things had to have had an ultimate non-contingent cause. But so far we've only considered physical things and physical forces acting on them. There are "things" that aren't physical at all, but are no less real for that. For example, we say that 2 plus 2 equals four, but this is an abstraction, not a physical thing. And yet, it is real. Moreover, the "thing" that is the equation $2 + 2 = 4$ is not in any way contingent. It necessarily exists; it is not caused by some prior physical state, in fact it is true irrespective of any physical state of the universe.

Though uncaused itself, the "thing" that is $2 + 2 = 4$ could be said to "cause" physical states, in that it (along with all mathematical statements) is information necessary to the existence of the universe. One might object that such information merely describes the workings of the universe, rather than causes them, but either way, the non-physical reality is necessary to the physical reality, as well as existing independently.

The mathematical ideals are not merely epiphenomena of physical things, nor "emergent" from physical states. Sometimes adherents to the philosophy of materialism will argue that phenomena not immediately explainable from matter in motion nonetheless "emerge" from matter, in the same sense that the image in a painting emerges from the application of differing pigments to canvas. For example, human consciousness, difficult to explain by naturalism, may be described as merely "emergent" from brain functioning. Either mind is in some degree affected by something other than the biology of the individual, or it is only a manifestation of the brain's functioning, so that immaterial elements of consciousness like willfulness, intentionality, continuity, unity, and subjectivity nonetheless "emerge" from the material brain. In the same way, real but non-physical virtues like courage and honor and honesty are said to emerge from the workings of the brain, and our perception of ideals like beauty, truth, and goodness likewise are a function of biology only. Real but non-physical reality is either entirely a human construct overlaid upon otherwise meaningless physical reality, or it is spoken by some entity into a chaos of nature to give it form and order.

The fact of these ideals is sometimes cited as the basis for the ontological argument for the existence of God. "Ontology" is that area of philosophy concerned with existence as such. The classic "ontological proof" of God is attributed to Anselm of Canterbury, from the eleventh century, but has been articulated by many previously, such as by Boethius, in his *Consolation of Philosophy* (fifth century). It's the idea that if we conceive of that for which there is nothing superior, we arrive at God. Inside this framework, we can suppose that for every physical thing, every virtue, and every ideal, we can move up the ladder, so to speak, to find a thing, virtue, or ideal that is better and better, moving on toward perfection. When we get to perfection, we must attach a name to it, and that name we attach is "God." So the idea is not that we preconceive a God and then try to prove He exists. Instead, we only conceive there is a point of perfection in every stream of thought about what constitutes the totality of reality. God's existence is the rational conclusion.

Subsumed into this concept of idealized perfection is the thinking of philosophers including pre-Christian pagan philosophers like Aristotle and Plato. Their conception of ideals supports the ontological proof of God's existence. Aristotle's *telos* conceives purpose even in merely physical things. For example, fire has a direction; it reaches up; its purpose is to heat and to consume. Stars purpose to move in a fixed pattern; animals purpose to procreate and provide for the next generation; the cells of the body work with like cells in the body to a common purpose. Gravity speaks to purposefulness in movement of material things. And so on.

The purpose apparent in physical reality seems to belie the necessary purposelessness of materialism. If there is any purpose whatsoever, the fact of purpose would point inexorably back to a provider of that purpose, One who designs purpose into physical things. But if all of physical nature is the unfolding of matter in motion according to physical forces, there is no purpose to any of it, it just is. Purpose does not exist as a brute fact of existence. If there is purpose in the movement of physical things, there would seem to be an entity, God, who provides purpose. If the actions and thoughts of people are merely the natural outworking of matter in motion, then the sense of purpose is entirely illusory. If human purpose is genuine, it is inconsistent with the dictates of materialism.

CHAPTER 5: IDEALS

While Aristotle pointed to actual, real existence, and the purposefulness of that real physical reality, Plato postulated a higher level of abstraction to mere physical reality, suggesting that physical reality is composed of specific instances of ideal forms. There is an ideal of a triangle, and of a horse, and every instance of a triangle or of a horse that we encounter is a specific and non-ideal instance of that perfect and ideal form. If you draw a triangle with chalk on a chalkboard, to illustrate a geometric theorem, you are not drawing a perfect triangle, but rather an imperfect representation of a perfect triangle. If you then show two sides as being a-squared and b-squared, respectively, and then the hypotenuse as being c-squared, you're demonstrating that relationship for an ideal triangle, not your real one. A student isn't going to come up and say "wait a minute, let's measure your drawn triangle sides and see if a-squared plus b-squared really equals the c-squared." Of course it won't. You didn't draw it perfectly, no one seriously thinks you're drawing anything but a representation of the ideal of a triangle. The theorem (the Pythagorean theorem) doesn't apply to your chalk triangle; only to the ideal one. The thing is, though, that the ideal triangle does not exist anywhere. It is not physical reality. The relationship of the sides of a right angle to a hypotenuse is a relationship that does not exist in physical reality, either. It applies only to the form of a triangle. So you have a real, physical world, and an ideal world of perfection. The same thing applies for a horse. When we see a horse, we recognize it as such based on a conception of the ideal horse in our mind. The real horses we encounter are imperfect instances of the ideal horse.

Augustine of Hippo lived half a millennium after Plato and Aristotle and was a Christian, but he was heavily influenced by Plato's idea of the forms, because it showed him this: that the ideal triangle and the ideal horse are part of reality just like real triangles and real horses. It is because of the reality of the ideal triangle that we can do geometry. It is because of the reality of the ideal horse that we can identify a real horse. If we know only of the family's farm horse and then encounter the neighbor's stallion, we still recognize both as horses. (It's also the reason we recognize a fetus or a mentally disabled person as human beings made in the image of God, and not something to be disposed of). Because the ideal triangle is part of reality but not part of physical reality, that means reality is comprised not just of physical things, but also by something more.

It might be said that both triangles and horses are physical things, and saying that there is an ideal of those physical things does not mean that there is anything other than physical things. But this concept applies also to that which is unassailably real, yet not manifested in physical form in any way. Like virtue. Honesty, bravery, justice, even truth, are all things that we can absolutely say exist, even though there is no physical counterpart to them at all. So it simply cannot be true that all of reality consists only of physical things. A skeptic might argue that honesty, bravery, and justice are things that evolved somehow, but he can't say they're not real. And though they're real, they're obviously not physical.

The subjective appreciation of physical things, such as revulsion or the rapturous response to beauty, is also real, and yet not physical. Beauty is a non-physical but real thing. It is like a virtue, in that regard. One might say beauty is subjectively experienced and evolved in mankind over time, but it is certainly real. Not only is beauty in the abstract a non-physical reality, but it is something we all recognize. Though there are variations in taste, there is not a completely separate conception of beauty in every single person. There's a reason that we recognize superlatives. You might love to hear a particular singer, for example, but it's not just you. The singing would be beautiful independent of your particular receptivity. Music aficionados may get together and argue about who's the best fiddle player, because they recognize the concept that someone could be the best at approaching perfection in fiddle-playing. Why? Plato might say there is an ideal of fiddle playing, and our favorite fiddle players are our favorites because they come closest to the pure form of fiddle-playing. When you hear a good musician play, you experience a moment of what we describe as "transcendence." If you have a religious bent at all, you might say that you feel close to God in that moment of pure musical perfection. It sounds "heavenly." And you'd be right, it's "heavenly" because heaven corresponds to that arena of perfection in which resides our concept of pure music. All real music is a reflection of that Platonic form. You feel close to God because what you are sensing is that you are getting nearer to that which is pure ideal rather than the physical reality of percussing sound waves with differing pitch and duration. You're perceiving that form behind real music, which is non-physical reality.

So there is physical reality, of course. But there is non-physical reality, too. And what's more, the non-physical reality encompasses or surrounds or embraces physical reality. Actual music, and honesty, and triangles are manifestations of the non-physical ideals of music and honesty and triangles. That's why you may experience a moment of transcendence when you hear great music. You hear the pure and non-physical ideal coming through in the playing of actual, physical music. The ideal could not exist if physical reality were all there is. Nor could the physical reality exist, if the ideal did not.

If there is an ideal of music, and of beauty, and of honesty, and bravery, and justice, and even truth, then doesn't logic take us to an Author of those ideals? There must be an explanation for the existence of these ideals; of Plato's forms, and that actualizing explanation must be something that is an ideal to the ideal, so to speak. The ideals are perfect: perfect music, perfect beauty, perfect triangles, and so on. Perfection in the abstract is itself is an ideal which stands behind and gives meaning to the more specific ideals. You might say physical music is at one level; the musical ideal is at the next level; and perfection in the abstract is at yet another level. Perfection is the ideal from which the ideals of perfect music, triangles, and horses derive. Perfection is the Form of the forms, so to speak. It is, in Anselm's formulation: "that than which nothing greater can be thought:" God.

Chapter 6: **Order**

In Nature

WHY IS THERE ORDER instead of chaos? Why do things happen in a predictable way? The orderliness of our physical environment is so much a part of our day-to-day experience that it takes some effort to imagine a world without it. What if, when you dropped something, it sometimes "fell" up instead of down? Suppose water ran uphill, but only sometimes? What if the air in some places settled out into very different concentrations of oxygen and nitrogen than what we are used to breathing? Or was composed of different elements altogether, from one place to another? Suppose the sun began rising at random times and the days varied in length to be less than or more than 24 hours. The orderliness of our environment is so much a part of our operating assumptions about reality that we cannot fully conceive of its absence.

The fact of orderliness in our universe means the natural processes in play are consistent. If an apple separates from the tree, it will fall to the earth rather than fly off into the sky. We expect that, and now we understand that it is the result of gravity, one of the fundamental natural forces in the universe. Any matter is reducible to a small number of kinds of tiny particles, and those particles have the same characteristics wherever they exist in the same combinations. The natural forces (gravity, electromagnetism, strong and weak nuclear forces) operate on matter in predictable ways; that is, they don't vary in strength or effect. In identical physical situations, these forces will act on physical objects in identical ways. We say these forces are predictable because they consistently follow describable patterns, according to consistent laws of physics.

This orderliness enables us to conceive of matter as existing in three physical dimensions: width, height, depth. Accordingly, we can chart the relative location of physical things mathematically, on a chart with three axes, conventionally denominated x, y, and z. We can think of time as a

CHAPTER 6: ORDER

fourth dimension, which sweeps along the other three in one "direction." The physical nature of time is but little understood, but it is a physical phenomenon, like the space dimensions. An object in a particular x, y, and z location at one time may be at another x, y, and z location at another time. Movement is detectable as occurring within a given span of consistently measurable time.

We can say the physical universe is composed of matter in motion because even a rock sitting unmoved for thousands of years is being borne along by the earth, which is moving, and in addition the rock is composed of moving atoms which are in turn composed of moving subatomic particles. All the matter of the universe and the forces acting upon it inside of time are orderly, meaning that we can apply the physical laws of nature to study and understand the characteristics of the matter and forces so we can say what will happen next.

We expect the sun to come up tomorrow because we understand that the earth is turning in relation to the sun in a consistent cycle. We can say, in advance, precisely when the sun will appear to crest the horizon from the vantage point of a particular place on the surface of the earth. Another way to describe this orderliness is to speak of the earth's movement relative to the sun as a *natural* process. The movements of earth and sun, as influenced by other material in space, proceeds in a predictable way. The fact of this proceeding—the *process*—is natural. That is, we can say that each movement of matter is caused by some other physical movement. For example, the earth turns just so because it was set in motion long ago, and continues on its path and at its speed as a result of natural forces acting upon it.

Source of Order

Order in the natural world is cited as evidence by both theists and materialists, though their points of view are mutually exclusive. On the one hand, the order of the universe is thought to support the idea that nature is all there is. On the other hand, the order of the universe is thought to prove the existence of an order-Creator outside the natural order.

Many people now think naturalism follows from the fact that natural processes explain so much. The more we can explain scientifically, the more likely it seems that science explains everything. So much of what seemed like mysteries from the realms of the gods in ages past are easily explainable as the result of natural processes. Angry gods don't cause volcanoes to erupt. They're caused by upward movement of extreme subterranean heat, perhaps in turn caused by tectonic shifts. One could point to gaps in scientific knowledge to assert the gaps exist because of the mysteries of God. To many minds, the more science closes those gaps, the more God is squeezed out. The thought is that whatever explanatory gaps remain will in time be naturally explained. In this way, materialism-of-the-gaps replaces God-of-the-gaps thinking. Both are invalid, however.

The fact of order is evidence of a theist point of view, too. People have known forever, even in the most ignorant, fearful, superstitious, and credulous times of history, that there are natural processes at work around us all the time. We have to look no further than the complex but quite natural process of human insemination and birth. Obviously the "how" of embryo formation and gestation was not always fully known, but clearly there was a natural process involved, commencing with sexual congress of male and female. We've always known where babies come from; that they're not really delivered by storks. We've always known that there are natural processes in play, even when the scope of our natural knowledge was much narrower than it is now. The point is that if the fact of natural processes somehow proved that nature is all there is, then it would be so proven for all people in history. People didn't incline to theism just because they didn't understand nature.

The fact of order within that nature suggested an order-creator; that it took a God to create the universe we know rather than a universe of chaos. Natural order is mindless, and could not have created itself, so it took Mind apart from the ordered universe to create it. If it were somehow self-created, coming into being without Mind attending it, or if it had somehow always existed, it would more likely exist in a state of chaos rather than order.

In Enlightenment times, from say the seventeenth century, science took major steps forward because the fact of order in the universe became better understood. We became better at understanding why things happen the way they do based on orderly natural forces following consistent and predictable physical laws. Science proceeded on the assumption of natural order — not that nature was all of reality, but that God ordained order for his creation. Further, that the Mind of God existed apart from that creation. At least in the West, it was understood that the mind of God did not enliven the physical things themselves.

To do science, however, it was not necessary to understand the nature of the relation between God and his creation. It was sufficient to grasp the

CHAPTER 6: ORDER

orderliness of physical things and of physical forces acting on them. The method of science assumes natural order without attempting to explain its source. This is sometimes referred to as "methodological naturalism," meaning scientists proceed as if all of reality is explainable physically. Spiritual reality, if it exists at all, could be left with the theologians, it simply was not the subject of science. It still isn't.

Science has unveiled much about our physical universe. For many it has to come to fill the imagination, leaving no room for other kinds of knowing. In this way, methodological naturalism is allowed to morph into philosophical naturalism. Science is a methodology for discovering truth about physical things, but is wrongly taken to mean instead the materialist conclusion that physical things are all of existence. Because materialism is in conflict with theism, the thinking would go that science and religion stand in opposition. That conclusion is the product of confused thinking, however. The confusion is readily dispelled with a basic understanding of what science is, and a general understanding of history and religion.

The predictability of physical movement of matter makes science possible. If all the movement of matter through space and time were unpredictable and random, there would be no way to draw conclusions about physical processes. Nature would be chaotic and its study would be pointless. Because there is order in the universe, however, we can study it. Through science we acquire ever greater understanding of the physical universe. There are different concentrations among scientists, of course, which is why we have disciplines of chemistry, biology, geology, and so on. Some of these scientific disciplines are more pragmatic, such as agronomy, and some are more basic, like physics. But all of them involve the study of the orderly physical universe.

All of science presupposes the existence of this order. Science *assumes* there are constant and measurable forces acting upon physical things in predictable ways. The very fact of order in the universe implies the existence of an order-giver. C.S. Lewis wrote: "Men became scientific because they expected Law in Nature, and they expected Law in Nature because they believed in a Legislator."* It has often been argued that Christianity provided the intellectual foundation for all of science, including its breakout in the early Enlightenment period with Francis Bacon, Isaac Newton, and others. Christianity provided this foundation because Christians envisioned a God

---

*Lewis, *Miracles* (1947) p. 110.

of order, who created material reality in a state of order, but who exists apart from that order.

If there is no God, however, then this matter in motion, responding to forces of nature, constitutes all of reality. A person who believes there is no God is a materialist; a naturalist; an anti-theist or atheist; one who rejects metaphysics. This is the dominant view of reality in our culture, and the point of view people necessarily adopt when they shrug the shoulders and ask "who knows" when considering the proposition that God is. If all of reality is natural reality, how does that vision of reality explain the obvious order of the universe? The short answer, for theists, is that it doesn't. Materialism depends on the existence of that order, but does not explain it.

The fact of order in the universe is important evidence about what constitutes all of reality. That evidence can be misunderstood, however, if we're not careful. Order is not necessarily evident from the fact that an apple falls toward the earth. But order *is* evident from the fact that *all* apples *always* fall to the earth. They always fall with the same velocity and acceleration given the mass of the object (the earth) toward which they fall and elements of resistance between tree and ground. Is the presence of this order a brute fact of existence? Or does it mean something beyond itself? The question is not why apples fall from trees in predictable ways. The answer to that question is gravity. The real question is: why is there gravity? And why does it behave the way it does? Why are there strong and weak nuclear forces, and electromagnetism? And a small number of elements with element-specific behaviors that comprise every known material thing in the universe?

It is useful to think of order as an independent phenomenon; that is, not as the sum of specific instances in which order is manifested, but rather order in the abstract. Not just the physical force of gravity acting consistently on physical things, but that there are consistent physical forces at all. Why is there order? Again, the question is not why things are the way they are. The answer to that is order: consistent physical forces acting on finite physical things in consistent ways. Our question is: why is there order?

Fine-tuning

A feature of nature that has been observed and commented on only recently (that is, say within the last 100 years or so) is the so-called "fine-tuning" of the universe. The idea is that slight changes in many of the mathematical

CHAPTER 6: ORDER

constants for physical phenomena would be catastrophic to the order we observe. Various mathematical relationships inherent in that order had to be just so in order to sustain the order of the universe as we know it. In fact, even the slightest tweak in many of these constants would mean the universe would not exist at all. There are many mathematical constants that constitute this fine-tuning. If any of them fell outside a very narrow tolerance range, there would be no universe or no universe of duration like ours.

Examples cited by scientists include these. An alteration in any of the values for the fundamental forces of gravity, electromagnetism, and strong and weak nuclear forces would mean the universe wouldn't exist. Its existence similarly relies on the relative strengths of electromagnetism and gravity; the efficiency of hydrogen fusion; the relative importance of gravity and expansion energy of the universe; the ratio of the density of dark energy to the critical energy density of the universe (the cosmological constant); the ratio of gravitational energy required to pull a galaxy apart to the energy equivalent of its mass; the number of spatial dimensions in physical things. These are all significant cosmologically, but even considering more local examples, it is remarkable that things are as they are. Imagine how different the world would be if the range of temperatures at which water remains in liquid form were only slightly different.

The fine-tuning necessary for life is similarly dramatic. At one time it was thought that life must be possible on many of the millions upon millions of planets in the universe, because it was thought that distance from a similar sun and the constituents for water might be sufficient. It turns out that's only the beginning. For just one example, the mass of Jupiter in proximity to earth deflects asteroids that would otherwise snuff out life here. Our earth only exists in habitable form because of precise values fixed to hundreds of known parameters.

Many people believe the order of the universe is deeply significant because it didn't have to be this way, and in fact looking at the various mathematical relationships of the universe, it seems almost magically coincidental; that it couldn't have been this way unless there was a designer of it: God. Physicist Freeman Dyson expressed it this way: "The more I examine the universe and the details of its architecture, the more evidence I find that the universe in some sense must have known we were coming."* In physicist Paul Davies' words: "We were truly meant to be

---

*Dyson, *Disturbing the Universe* (1979) p. 250.

here."* In addition to the significance of each of these constants, there is the significance of all of them combined making the present universe and life within it possible. The arithmetical significance jumps to the exponential, we might say, from the combination of all these finely-tuned variables. We wouldn't be here to have this conversation if the cosmological mathematical relationships were not just so.

There are materialist responses to this. Chief among them is the anthropic principle, the idea that the mathematical information yielded by cosmology is not coincidental at all, but exists as it does by virtue of the fact that we are doing the observing, and observation by beings such as ourselves would not be possible if the universe were not orderly in just the way it is. Only in a universe capable of eventually supporting life will there be living beings capable of observing and reflecting on it.

The anthropic principle is true as far as it goes, but it seems to get the matter backward. Yes a precisely-tuned universe is being observed by people who are made possible by the existence of the precisely-tuned universe, but that does not dispel the coincidence that the entire cosmos just happens to be constructed on such precise tolerances that it not only continues in existence, but supports life, including sentient life, at least on earth.

Another materialist response is that this precisely-tuned universe need not be the only universe; that perhaps innumerable others are differently "tuned." This is multiverse theory, the idea that there are numerous, perhaps infinite universes, and that only this one is "tuned" the way it is, so there is no coincidence involved. The thought is that other universes may have differing features, in differing mathematical relationship, so that they are born and quickly die, or exist without supporting life.

Multiverse theory comes into discussion in other contexts, too, such as in attempts to explain quantum phenomena that seem to be at odds with relativity. If true, the multiverse would mean that our word "universe" is a bad label; that all of physical reality includes not just the cosmos we know (the limits of which are already speculative) but others as well. That doesn't mean multiverse theory is wrong, but even if it were discovered to be true, it would not adequately explain the goldilocks phenomenon of this one. All appearances are, still, that the universe is the way it is because it was designed this way. And if it was designed this way, there had to be a Designer.

---

*Davies, *Mind of God: The Scientific Basis for a Rational World* (1993) p. 232.

CHAPTER 6: ORDER

Information

It has occurred to many scientists and philosophers that the mathematical relationships extant in the universe are a kind of information, much like the encoded biological information in DNA. This perspective immediately suggests the existence of an intelligent information provider. In the cosmology context, the information would include this mathematical "tuning" which causes the universe not only to be what it is, but to be—period. The mathematical relationships are necessary to tune the universe to exist and to exist in such manner that life is possible, at least in this little corner. Regarding these mathematical relationships as information immediately suggests a sentient provider of that information. In the case of DNA in biological organisms, the obvious coded information is explained away—however unpersuasively—as the result of deselection of coded bits in predecessor carriers of the information over time. No such explanation is available for the encoding of the universe, however. There is no iterative process one could theorize to passively develop the information, as with the theory of naturalistic evolution.

Chapter 7: **Disorder**

The Broken World

DESPITE THE EVIDENT NATURAL order of the universe, people down through the ages have had an intuition that the world seems not right, entirely. It seems in a sense compromised, or broken in some way. That intuition is behind a Christian perspective. It is why the Bible speaks of the moral fall of mankind as central in the creation story, and also the fall in the created order around mankind. Christ's mission is understood to redeem mankind, but also to make all things new in his time.

But suppose this intuition is misplaced. Perhaps there was no state of perfect order that is corrupted to what we experience. How might materialism explain our sense of "evil" in the context of naturally-occurring bad things happening to people, or "evil" in the sense of intentional acts of moral wrong perpetrated against others?

We would do well to pause and consider why we have this sense of brokenness. We think of it as a deviation from a state of affairs we regard as whole or perfect or complete. We would consider a world without natural disaster or evil or death to be such a world, but why? Why aren't the disruptions of fire and flood just as good as their absence? Why is death a sad thing? Why do we regard violence against others to be evil—or said differently, where does the notion of evil come from in the first place?

To understand the materialist worldview in light of this sense of disorder, we first have to put aside the Christian idea that there was harmony between God and his creation, including people, "in the beginning." We have to imagine the world did not somehow become broken; that it has always been this way: natural disasters, violence, disease, death. That means the current status quo is normal.

Further, any intuition we may have that there is a broken-ness to the world is a false signal, something evolved into us to enhance survival, but not necessarily true. If we are born with any information content,

CHAPTER 7: DISORDER

like fear or wariness or desire, that information content is not necessarily true, because it derives solely from evolution, which is driven by survival, not truth. It may be false, yet serve to enhance survival. This intuition of disorder in the world would be just such a false feeling, because materialism negates the disorder hypothesis. There would be no such thing as disorder, if materialism is a true understanding of reality. And yet, we perceive (and intuit) disorder.

If materialism explains all of reality, then our experience of physical reality is entirely normal. If so, then why would we attach the word "evil" to anything that happens? Hate would not be evil, it would be normal. As would death, disease, natural disaster, rape, pillage, plunder, war. If we imagine this existence to be entirely normal because all these bad things just unfold naturally from the movement of material particles in time, then we should disregard any feeling of unease resulting from it. We should immediately scrap our entire criminal justice system. The intuition of disorder would be something we can overcome by the exercise of reason, if it is only a vestigial emotion wrought by evolution. If naturalism is an accurate understanding of reality, there is no disorder.

The physical death we all must suffer at the end of our time-bound existence would seem to be a rather obvious symptom of a broken world. But the very ubiquity of this phenomenon lulls us into regarding it as a normal physical process. We can come to think of death of the body as being a natural physical process like the changing of the tide. So perhaps a better illustration of the problem is with some bad thing that is not so universal. Perhaps an untimely death of an entire family, including children, in a horrible car crash. Or a stillborn child. Or a child born with physical limitations that will cause the child to suffer physically all its days. That should be regarded by us as being just as normal, if everything mankind experiences is the result of natural processes and nothing else. But we can't help a feeling of empathy with a person so afflicted, and with that empathy, a sense of unfairness or darkness or, again: disorder.

It turns out that every person alive actually is born with an affliction, but it's not a physical one, it's spiritual. The Christian way of describing this affliction is "sin." Our moral compass is prone to deviate from true north. It's a recurring problem, and it's not something we can unilaterally fix. It's a burden to us. It inhibits our freedom. But precisely because of its ubiquity, we have a tendency to ignore it or unthinkingly ascribe it to nature; as a natural thing just like death. The Christian view is that it is not just the world that is broken; it is ourselves. Or perhaps said better, the brokenness of the world originates with me. It actually is a "natural" condition, but not in the way adherents of naturalism mean.

On a deep level we depend on the orderliness of the cosmos to make sense of the world and of our places in it. At the same time we have to recognize the pervasive *disorder*. This is not to say that, despite prevailing natural order, chaos randomly takes over and renders physical processes suddenly incomprehensible. This disorder does not mean a temporary breach in the laws of physics or a random change-up in physical forces or the make-up of material things. Rather, "disorder" includes: (a) accidents and natural disasters that are tragic to particular people, especially in circumstances that seem chaotic, or are unexpected, or are otherwise inexplicable; (b) death and disease; and (c) evil as it is perpetrated by people against other people.

Natural Disaster

The usual way of thinking about accidents and natural disasters is that though they may be tragic, they're nobody's "fault;" they're just things that happen. Flood, hurricane, avalanche, fire, volcano. Still, we tend to think of them as aberrations; as events outside the proper workings of the world. In times past they might have been ascribed to some sort of divine retribution for the victims. But we know natural catastrophic events to be, as far as we can tell, natural processes caused by other natural processes. As we come to understand them better we can undertake measures to mitigate their effects in advance, precisely because of improvement in our understanding of the natural processes behind them.

These natural disasters are not like the usual progression of disease and then death, from the winding-down of the life-cycle, because that feature of human existence seems endemic to our condition—what it means to be human. Accidents and natural disasters are also usually considered distinct from instances of evil: occasions in which a being with moral agency perpetrates hardship or loss on another. Again, they are endemic to the physical environment in which we live; in fact we can say they evince disorder rather than order only because they are difficult to predict and may result in loss of life and property. They are not typically considered instances of evil.

But why not? If there is a God, might we consider the "fault" for such events to lie at his feet? Perhaps so, if we understand him as being sovereign over his creation such that nothing happens outside his control. Even

CHAPTER 7: DISORDER

accidents and natural disasters would thereby be evil that God permits, if not causes. Storms, fires, floods, epidemics, and other bad things happening to people might seem unfair, and therefore imbued with some sort of wrongful intent, though the direct causes are innumerable natural processes building each upon the other until the volcano blows, or the tsunami comes ashore, or the wildfire sweeps into inhabited areas.

Thus, accidents and natural disasters might be placed in the category of "evil"—intentional wrongs perpetrated against people—which exist as a kind of disorder in the world. We might conclude that God is therefore not all-good. We could go on to conclude that if he is not all-good, then he doesn't fit our conception of God, so perhaps there is no God at all. But that kind of thinking is circular. Either he exists or he doesn't. Only if he exists in the first place might we consider pinning natural disasters on him as a form of evil. If he doesn't exist, then natural disasters result solely from natural processes, and so there is no "evil" associated with them, they just are.

If God is responsible for accidents and natural disasters that harm people, can we say that he participates in evil? Evil must be regarded as intentional wrong perpetrated on innocent people. We wouldn't say, for example, that killing in self-defense is evil. A thing is evil only if the victims are deemed innocent. Orthodox Christianity teaches that no one is. That's a radical thought in the current cultural climate, but it's no less true for that. Still, most people don't think of harm to people through accidents and natural disasters as being instances of evil. We view this evidence as a sort of inevitable defect in the order of things, in the same way we think of the natural winding down of human life.

Death

The fact of disorder in the world is perhaps nowhere more obvious than in this central, defining fact about our existence: We are all dying. If we want to complain about the nature of God's creation, that would seem to be the starting place, but we don't generally point a finger of accusation at God because we die. Instead, we think of it as a natural process, in the same way we think of the changing of the leaves, and rainfall, and birth. As bad as it is, we are reconciled to the fact of death. We tend not to think of it as a source of disorder in the world, but why wouldn't we?

If there is a supernatural reality, it would be presumed to provide the answer: that this physical and temporary life is in some way preparation for what lies beyond it. And the converse: that life in a timeless supernatural realm provides meaning and purpose in this temporal one. The spiritual realm implies purpose in this natural one, and these conclusions are necessary to finding purpose to life despite our inevitable death.

In the naturalism paradigm, by contrast, people are natural processes like everything else, all with a finite life-span. The lives of plants and animals are initiated after the pattern of their kind, and after a season of juvenile development operate optimally, for the central part of their lifetimes. Then senescence creeps in until the process wears out and its elements return inert to the environment. Over millenia the populations of the various organic processes change form and become more complex, but there is no meaning or purpose to it, nor any goal to the development of an individual or population.

Evil

In addition to this natural disordered state in the cosmos, there is rather obviously something wrong with people. We are selfish, lustful, malevolent, hateful—the list goes on and on. We might not consider drowning in a flood to be the result of "evil," but we don't hesitate to see evil in murder. Even in the case of murder, however, is it really the result of evil? If a person is a natural process just like any other; if he has no moral agency and therefore no moral responsibility, then why wouldn't the thoughts and actions leading to the murder be considered natural processes, too? Why would we consider it "evil," in other words, rather than just another natural event like a hurricane?

Given this feature of the materialist paradigm, can we speak intelligibly of evil? Routinely, people who advocate for materialism point to the fact of evil as disproving God. The proposition is that God would not allow evil, but we have evil, therefore there is no God. As is so often the case, however, the rejoinder requires taking a step back to examine assumptions. The assumption behind the argument is that good and evil as we know them can exist in a God-less reality. Can that be true?

Of course we know what evil is, because we have a moral sense. Materialists could argue that the moral sense is a result of evolved intuition about conduct that is desirable and undesirable, and further, that evolution results in a doubling down on this intuition such that we attach

CHAPTER 7: DISORDER

honor and shame to intuitions of what would otherwise be merely desirable and undesirable.

But let's think about that. It would mean that earlier populations of humans had a larger proportion of individuals with a lesser-developed moral sense, and over time, those individuals with a more developed moral sense were more likely to survive, for reasons of social acceptance, such that the population of humans consisted of a progressively higher proportion of individuals with a progressively more developed moral sense.

Fine, so far, that's basic evolutionary theory. But it means this thing we're calling a moral sense (or a conscience) is actually just content-laden brain biology that developed *to enhance survivability*. We call something morally "right" or "wrong," but to be consistent with naturalism, we ought to call it instead "fitness-enhancing" or its opposite. That would mean the moral intuition exists only because it enhanced survival, not because it is, objectively, morally right or wrong.

Because moral "good" and "evil" are just words we attach to conduct associated with enhanced or reduced survivability, there would actually be no moral component to it at all. "Evil" as such would not exist, and so it is senseless to say anything is evil given the naturalism paradigm. Invoking "evil" to disprove God doesn't work because without God there is no basis for assigning moral "good" or "evil" to anything. Bad things happen just because they do; it's the natural out-working of all the movement of atoms in space from the beginning of time. "Good" and "evil" have no place in a God-less universe. In the atheist worldview, there is no fundamental brokenness to the world, as with the Christian fall of man. There is no ideal, therefore, from which deviations could be called "evil." In the materialist worldview there is no "problem" of evil, because *there is no evil*. Nor good. Instead of referring to theists' "problem of evil," it makes more sense to refer to atheists' problem of good.

It is only in the theistic worldview that we consider the world in some way broken, such that "evil" results, and "good" may come from choices we have the moral freedom to make. Given the theist worldview, why and how does God tolerate evil? The first answer is: Ask God. Seriously, we're already out of bounds if we're questioning why God does or does not do something. He does what he jolly well pleases. We can make inferences about the nature of God from what we observe about his exercise of sovereignty over his dominion, and we can even, in our position of limited understanding, dislike him so much that we shake the fist at him. But our evaluation of him does not cancel his very existence. We can't hold God to our standards. He holds us to his. That's what it means for us to be us, and God to be God.

We can reconcile what we know with the fact of evil in a couple of different ways. First, it is true that God is absolute good. He defines good and embodies good, He doesn't merely do things we recognize as good. We should be conscious, therefore, that we miss the point entirely if we assign evil to acts or omissions of God. He defines what is good, so if we attribute evil to God, we do so by defining good and evil ourselves, and then comparing God to the standard we come up with. That's backwards. If we think God is dabbling in evil, it's on us to reevaluate what we call good and evil, rather than indicting God.

It has to be said that God does "tolerate" evil, but only in the sense that evil exists in his domain and he could certainly extinguish it if he wanted to. But he doesn't "tolerate" it in the sense that people often misuse the word "tolerate" now. We've essentially turned the word (the word "tolerate") upside down, to mean that we are to accept and approve the thing we say we're tolerating; in other words, to agree with its being proper conduct, rather than holding to what the word actually means: withholding censure despite disagreement.

But even with the correct understanding of "tolerance," why would God tolerate evil? If God is absolute good, and anything else is not-God, then anything besides God is going to be something less than absolute good. We know in our bones that we exist in a moral universe, and further, that we fail morally, individually and collectively. Every movie, book, or play that involves any kind of written or spoken narrative is ultimately about moral questions. Our entire criminal justice system is based on the idea that we bear moral responsibility for what we do. It is about much more than sequestering dangerous people from the rest of society, and even that most basic purpose involves moral judgment. Unquestionably, human beings act in ways that we do not hesitate to call "evil." So why does God put up with us?

He doesn't. He holds us to his standards. And according to orthodox Christianity, he removes us from his presence if we are not reconciled to him. Because we cannot be reconciled to him on our own merits, given his purity and our lack, we must rely on him to reconcile us to himself. Those who cling to Jesus do so to escape the appropriate wrath of the Father. In this way, love overcomes evil. In this way people retain their freedom, including their moral freedom, but do not have to remain condemned in their morally responsible but not-God state.

God could have created a world without evil, but it would require creating mankind with no moral freedom. We would not exist, or would exist only as a race of beings not recognizably us. The existence of evil in the world actually proves the special-ness of human beings. We have agency to choose good, or to choose evil. It matters to God what we do, but it matters even more that we have the freedom to choose. It obviously matters a great deal to God that we behave rightly, and yet he desires our freely-given love so much that he gave us freedom to choose wrongly. Moral freedom proves God's desire for communion with us, rather than mere obedience. If we don't embrace the entirety of this relationship, it's easy to think of God as aloof and unsmiling, ready to smite us upon our deaths. But if we consider his restraint, during our lifetime, and his sustaining of the world by his vast reservoir of love, and his unilateral provision of the means of escaping judgment, we should see the extraordinary steps he takes to hold on to us, so that we cannot fairly consider him aloof at all.

Our moral freedom means that what we do in life is hugely significant. We often misunderstand freedom. We tend to think of it as a positive good, seeing nothing negative about it. Genuine freedom means freedom to fail as well as to succeed, however. Or to say it differently, if success was the only possible outcome of the exercise of our freedom, it wouldn't be freedom at all. It may seem appealing to abdicate moral responsibility and relax into the minimal moral standards of the current zeitgeist. It might seem freeing to throw off the success/failure paradigm of moral responsibility. This drift would seem to remove the negative weight of moral decision-making, but it removes the positive significance, too. It's a matter of giving up the highs and lows; becoming morally insensitive. But that's not genuine freedom, it's only a misguided trade-off. Ultimately it doesn't work. It doesn't remove the weightiness of our moral decision-making. Our freely-made moral choices determine our future, both in this life and in the life to come.

Chapter 8: **History**

It's tempting when we're young to think history is irrelevant. Perhaps it would be better if the world starts anew with me and my generation, we think. It's easy to think of history as little more than a series of unfortunate misadventures, if we bog down in battles and treaties and kings and the like. More interesting is the history of ideas, the prevalent beliefs and attitudes that really guide the course of human events.

Most people realize, though perhaps only gradually, that we can't be severed from the influences of history. Rather, we're caught up with it ineluctably, so that we don't see the innumerable impacts all the moments of history bring to bear on the operating assumptions of our lives. Why do we dress the way we do? Eat what we eat? Speak the language we speak? More fundamentally, why do we think the thoughts we think?

Religious ideas evolved differently in the East and the West. In the East, there was the idea that a divine presence exists in things, and people, so that physical things, including people, are somehow steeped in or derived from or emergent from the universal divine Mind. In the West, there developed a conception of deity independent from people and things. We will focus on the West, because, for good or ill, we live in a culture most predominantly Western in origin. To understand on the largest possible scale the history of ideas on the subject matter concerning us here, what follows is a (very condensed) history of western civilization in three epochs: the pagan, the Christian, and the materialist.

Pagan Epoch

In early agrarian societies ancestors were revered to such an extent that families would "keep the home fires burning," in constant devotion to the family's ancestors. Those ancestors were thought in some way to remain with the family, tied to them quite locally, buried on the grounds of the household and in that way continuously tied to the family. As generations passed, this ancestor worship evolved to worship of family gods, still quite local to a family, which then was not mom, pop, and kids, but rather extended sets of relations: a small tribe. When a wife was taken from a neighboring tribe, she would not continue to honor her family's god(s), but would thenceforth honor her husband's. She was carried over the threshold of the new family's house as an act of rejection of the old gods, and embrace of the new. The worship of family gods was tied to devotion to the place in which the tribe's ancestors were buried.

Over time, this devotion to the tribal gods evolved further. The venerated locality for the tribe might grow to accommodate more tribes, perhaps progressively less closely related to the original tribe. A multiplicity of family gods gave way to a god or gods of the locality. Devotion to the city and its inhabitants under the city's gods replaced over time devotion to the tribe's god and the tribe's devotion to the locality of its home. At this stage of history we begin to understand the devotion of, for example, the characters in classical writings to the place of their birth, and to the city, and to the city's gods.

To make sense of this in the context of other religious beliefs (like that of the Jews, and of later Christianity) one must pause and consider what the worldview of pagans was. They believed in multiple gods, of course, just as we see with the Greek and then Roman pantheons, and the Norse gods. Such a god was not the one necessary creator-god, but rather what might be referred to as a *demiurge;* a god with super-human but limited authority and power. They were thought to have personalities, including human-like traits and foibles. They were initially associated with specific places, specific cities, on earth. Histories of god-to-god interaction were imagined for them, and sometimes that interaction was mischievous, cruel, or scheming. A moral sense was not necessary to gods, though good moral traits were attributed to many of them. Importantly, they were not worshipped in the same way that Jews or Christians or Muslims worship God. It would be more accurate to say they were honored, by the upholding of certain prescribed rites and practices. As long as one "honored the gods" by completing these rites and following these practices, he was at peace with the gods of the city of which he was a part. The fabric of society was held together, by common observance of these rites.

Within this context, we make sense of the story of Socrates' death in 399 B.C. He was tried and convicted, and put to death, for refusing to honor the city's gods. The story of Socrates' trial is the triumph of reason over what is merely customary. Socrates was tried because he commended critical reasoning rather than rote acceptance of customary morality. In those days, derogation from the communal polytheistic observances was an affront not merely to religion, but to the integrity of society. Socrates said that he honored the gods more profoundly than those who engaged only in ritualistic observances. He acknowledged one over-arching god, an entity that was more significant than the Greek gods, though also apparently not the exclusive and personal God of the Hebrews.

In the centuries before the advent of the Christ, philosophers acknowledged the necessity of a creator agent outside of the creation. It was the point of Plato's forms, that there be an eternal and ideal form for the things and ideas that we work with in this life. Aristotle discussed reality in his formal and final causes, imputing a *telos*, or purposeful direction, to matter and time. Thus a god that was more than a mere demiurge was conceived as a philosophical necessity: the uncaused-cause; the agency outside of the material world which creates the world and the physical laws by which it operates; the ultimate reality of which physical things in space and time are mere shadows.

While these ideas developed in the pagan world, God is reported as speaking in the medium of history, through his prophets, in one tribal people, the Hebrews. King David, a type of the coming Christ, lived in about 1,000 BC. Moses led the people out of Egypt 500 or so years before that. Abraham was blessed by God another 500 or so years before that. The God of the Hebrews was understood to be the great creator-God, not a demiurge of pagan imagining. Unlike the philosophically necessary God of the Greek philosophers, however, the God of the Hebrews was a personal God.

It was from this chosen people of God that the Messiah came. He came first to the Jews, and then to the rest of the world. He and then his followers introduced this personal and ultimate God to the pagan world. In the pagan world it was taken for granted that there was an intelligent agency existing beyond the here-and-now of physical things and time. Pagans were not materialists. It was so much a part of the thinking of people at the time that when Christians began breaking out of the Hebrew enclaves and speaking to the world at large of the one personal God, they were often reviled and rejected and persecuted as "atheists," because they rejected the demiurge gods that were thought to provide order to society, and worshipped only the one creator-God, manifested in the Trinity.

CHAPTER 8: HISTORY

People generally did not believe nature to be all there was, in the pagan world. When Christ came and His followers took the message to the world, they were taking it to the pagan world, not to materialists. The environment in which Christianity began to spread was among people who believed in supernatural agency already; not people who thought nature comprised all of reality. An "atheist" of those times would not be one who embraced materialism, but rather one who rejected the tribal gods, and by extension, one's local society.

Christian Epoch

The beginning of the Christian epoch of course traces to Christ's public ministry commencing in the late 20's AD, when he proclaimed his deity in a progressively more explicit manner. He was killed because of this claim, and according to orthodox Christian belief, rose from the dead—not metaphorically, but literally and bodily.

The spread of the message of Christianity was at first a word-of-mouth endeavor. The Jews heard the message through very different ears than the gentiles. They either rejected it as blasphemous, or understood it as the culmination of their history thus far, and accepted it on that basis. Gentiles heard it as a strange claim that there was but one God, the personal God of the Hebrews, with whom we have communion even here and now, and that he alone should be worshipped. Further, he was a different Being altogether than the demiurge of pagan imagining. Instead he was the very author of all Being, and fully righteous. In fact, his righteousness creates such a gap between himself and man that it is unbridgeable, without a means of redemption offered by God himself. Those who heard the Christian message and accepted it understood God as relational with us; a God in whom "we live, and move, and have our being." As the context of the quoted passage in Acts 17 reveals, this was a longing of mankind that predated the advent of the Christ, and was thought satisfied through the Advent and presence of the Holy Spirit in the world.

This was a sharply different way of thinking about supernatural reality. Rather than lesser deities engaged in human-like behavior, demanding rote execution of rites to assure peace with immortals, the former pagans declared fealty to the very Creator of all; the uncaused-cause and ultimate reality that their philosophers and their own instincts recognized. Moreover, this was a personal God, whose eye was on the sparrow, and who knew every hair on their heads. The testimony of those who had seen Jesus following the Resurrection was believed, and that meant that converts to the faith of Christianity responded to a deeply-felt recognition of the sacrifice that was made for their redemption. The deep desire of God for communion with man was manifested in this act, and the Resurrection was thought an irrefutable proof of a reality beyond the here-and-now, and disproof of the imagined gods who no longer held sway over them. Christianity was truly revolutionary, in a way that we can scarcely imagine today.

Christian symbolism of the time indicated the radical nature of this shift. Following the practice of Jews, and in contrast to the practices of pagans, Christians oriented their churches so they could face east in worship. This was in defiance of the pagan gods for whom temples were oriented to other directions. Catechumens to the early church were directed first to face west, the direction of death and darkness, to bitterly renounce the false pagan gods, and then turn east, the direction of morning and light and Christ's return, to embrace him. The word "east" is derived linguistically from "dawn," or even "resurrection," and of course refers to a point of the compass. This practice of eastward orientation to show renunciation of pagan gods and to embrace the one true God is reflected in the word attached to Christians' celebration of the Passover of the Lord's Resurrection: "Easter."

This is not to say that Christianity caught on instantly among former pagans, however. In fact there was a gradual expansion until such time as it achieved toleration among the wider world, finally becoming accepted generally in lands surrounding the Mediterranean. A Jewish diaspora commenced in the first century. Islam was founded in the early seventh century and its reach has ebbed and flowed over the intervening centuries.

Christianity grew despite its minority religion status and occasional persecution. Once accepted by secular rulers, most notably the Roman emperor Constantine in the early 4th century, the church grew explosively, but with much painful working out of a systematic theology. Christ's teaching had been by exposition, and example, and miracle-working. It was left to the church, and especially the first-century apostle Paul, to continue to think through the theological principles—as well as limited man might—to a systematic theology.

Through all of that, however, it was well understood that this was not the spread of beliefs of morally perfect people. It was the spread of understanding of how one is reconciled to God, despite imperfection. "Christendom" extended to its boundaries with Muslim and Eastern religions.

Despite schisms, the western world was mostly Christian, with an understanding that this meant Christian in belief, not necessarily achieving Christianity's aspirational moral standards.

In later years competing ideas were weighed and heresy was identified. The early church became centralized, and through schisms on theological points, became the Eastern Church and the Roman Church claiming authority over eastern and western Europe, respectively, with certain other early-founded churches never reconciled to either. In western Europe, a movement of Christians away from the authority of the Roman Catholic church gained momentum. An act by Martin Luther in 1517 is usually cited for the beginning of the Reformation, commencing further schisms among Protestant denominations and churches, which continues to this day.

Materialist Age

Today, the process of seeking God in history has slowed among large swaths of people-groups that in previous generations devotedly sought him. Human progress in arts and science and political theory, combined with skepticism concerning anything which does not present to our sense impressions, has shifted our attention from the Creator, to that which is created, especially man himself. Among many who do not disavow God altogether, the historicity of the Christian story, and especially the Resurrection, are deemed non-essential, or true only metaphorically. In general, the Christian claims to truth about God's character and man's have become obscured. There has been an erosion in understanding of what "faith" actually is, and of the essential truth claims of Christianity, and of the ways in which they diverge from the increasingly prevalent humanist orthodoxy. The Western world has become increasingly secular, politically, and the philosophy of materialism has progressed to the point that it now eclipses Christianity.

This has been an accelerating process over the last 300-plus years. We mark the "Enlightenment" period of history as commencing in the seventeenth or early eighteenth century. It was the beginning of a transition from the Christian epoch. The predominant Christian worldview began giving way to a belief that man's reason alone was the source of understanding. The idea was that one is "enlightened" because he is coming out of the darkness of religious superstition and obscurantism. Over time, Europe heard "the long withdrawing roar" of faith, as famously described in Matthew Arnold's poem *Dover Beach*.

Charles Darwin published his *On the Origin of Species* in 1859, regarded by many as warrant for naturalism, the belief that all of nature is self-creating and self-developing. By the late nineteenth century various "freethinker" movements had gained in popularity, even in the United States, which still to that point had a baseline of Christian belief and piety, broadly speaking. By the end of the demoralizing First World War, 1914-18, Christianity was much reduced in Europe, society-wide. It has been in decline since, if not as rapidly, in the United States.

In the twentieth century we saw conflicts which were not about power or territory or prestige or religious factionalism, but were driven by communism and national socialism and related variations of human social engineering, all premised on materialist ideology. The chief modern competitor of Christianity thus arrived on the scene in a wave of unprecedented bloodshed. Political systems based on materialist ideology were largely overcome, in the twentieth century, but the materialist worldview behind them continues to advance in the culture of the West. The prevalent materialism is twined with a form of humanism derived from certain features of Christianity but otherwise not resembling it. In the new humanism, certain moral principles derived from Christianity survive, though often in transmuted form. These include charity, love for one's fellow man, sharing material blessings, and personal aspiration to make a difference in society rather than simply to get ahead. Other Christian principles appear to be less a part of the new humanism, however, such as sexual rectitude, reverence, humility, and gratitude. Thus, some long-held Christian (and Jewish) principles for human behavior survive, but the metaphysical basis for them does not.

Rejection of monotheisms in the modern age is seldom followed by embrace of some other form of supernatural reality, like paganism or some form of Eastern pantheism. Instead, people who reject the God of the Bible typically reject the proposition of supernatural truth altogether. That is a default to materialism. Christianity is giving way to materialism. This trend is unmistakable, in the prosperous West. For individuals it usually takes the form of rejecting Christian claims, without first grasping the materialist doctrine to which one defaults, in doing so. The mistake is to think one backs away from Christianity into a zone of neutrality. It is common for people to reject theism but neglect to consider precisely what they necessarily accept in its place. There is a tendency to think in terms of a-theism, rather than materialism; that is, to announce what one doesn't believe, rather than what one does. A better way is to understand the competing visions of reality, and evaluate the evidence available to all of us to decide what is true.

Paganism gave way to theism, and theism gives way to materialism. And yet, many people don't have a working understanding of materialism, nor an understanding of its metaphysical implications. People default to materialism when they reject theism, without adequately considering it as a set of doctrines about the scope of reality. It is a stealth ideology, in that sense, unique in history for how it came to be the dominant ideology of metaphysics. It is mistaken for mere neutrality about religious doctrines.

This tendency to embrace a neutrality that doesn't exist is exacerbated by political developments in the West. The political principle of tolerance for competing beliefs has been difficult to effectuate, the more so to the extent societies become collectivist. In such societies government becomes ever more pervasive, with a resulting expectation of shared beliefs in humanist values. Those values collide with certain traditional Christian and Jewish values. The principle of toleration is deemed paramount, but toleration is taken to mean, paradoxically, acceptance of a secular humanist orthodoxy and rejection of its religious competitors.

In the United States, for example, the political principle of mutual toleration means a separation of church and state, which is in turn taken to mean religion can have nothing to do with any public enterprise. Exclusion of religious values from public undertakings does not leave a vacuum, but instead forces post-Christian humanist values on public undertakings. As government expands, public undertakings expand, and with them the derivative but secular post-Christian humanist values, rather than Christian values. At the same time, materialism drives culturally-shaped values, and those values include, alarmingly, an expectation of conformity—what is often referred to as "political correctness."

Direction

Some people think history is a random unfolding of events. Some think it has a direction or end-point, such that events follow each upon the other to such final end. The Christian perspective certainly holds that there is a direction to history. Christian eschatology is as important to its doctrine as ultimate origins. God has a plan in history, as we see from the Old Testament neon sign pointing to the advent of the Christ, and then the Resurrection, and the expectation of Christ's return. The direction to history is provided by God. The Bible records it dramatically unfolding to reveal the redeemer of the universe, the culmination of human history to the time of his Advent. And then a promise, that at an unspecified and very vaguely-described point in the future, Christ will return. But then the Bible ends with some teaching to the early church, and some apocalyptic vision that is difficult to understand, and the promise of God's persistent presence with us. Then the church goes forward, trying to make sense of it all and working out the significance of the Ascension and promise of Christ's return.

A criticism of this view is that Christianity leaves us with an understanding of hugely significant events followed by two thousand years of silence. Some study and understanding is appropriate, of what has unfolded since the time the Christ walked among us as a man. The searching after a systematic theology that makes for a comprehensible whole is invaluable, and it has taken a long time. It has also taken place within a context of flawed mankind working through a mix of motivations, ambitions, and appetites. The development of understanding of God's character and how he interacts with us and with physical reality is difficult, and it has caused schisms, most notably in the Reformation. But these are important developments, too. Christianity holds there is a direction to these historical developments, so the inference is that it is worthwhile for us to attempt to trace it out as best we can. In fact, it is ever more important that we understand God's movements in history, as time marches on. If Christian claims are true, every day that passes is a day closer to the day of the Lord.

Materialism logically follows the idea of a direction to history, too, but it presumes a ground-up direction, so to speak; one that inheres in the changes in physical things over time. If the naturalist origin story is that things just popped into existence and then coalesced over time into galaxies and humans and other physical things, then the physical state of everything at this moment is the result of all the movements of matter in the moment preceding, and everything then was the result of the moment before that, and so on backward to the first cause of all subsequent contingent causes. That means the future is similarly determined, because there is one and only one way for events to unfold from this day forward.

The orthodox Christian doctrine of predestination relates to this sense of direction to history. Predestination means God chose his own from the foundation of the world. So does this mean God orchestrates those events

CHAPTER 8: HISTORY

and all others, so everything's already decided? If everything is already decided, what's left for me to do?

At the same time, the Bible tells us we have moral agency; free will. It implies free will from start to finish. People are admonished to purity precisely because they feel, subjectively, that they can exercise their will in the direction of doing good or bad. We're told we ought to do good, but obviously we can choose to do bad. In fact, in the opening stories of creation we read of man's choosing bad, betraying God, as an act by which he acquires moral consciousness and becomes estranged from God, thereafter needing reconciliation which can only come from God.

How can both free will and predestination be true? And if they can't both be true, does that mean all the claims of Christianity are false?

If you read commentary on this question, it usually amounts to a long-winded way of saying it's a mystery how they can be reconciled, yet they must be. More far-reaching thought would seem to indicate that both are true, but as with so much else in the Bible that is puzzling, exactly how hinges on the nature of God, and in particular the ways in which he is different from us. We can know a good bit about human perspective, but very little, of course, about God's.

The entire inquiry relates to time. We tend to think of God having at one point in time foreknowledge of what will happen in the future. That's what the Bible says. But we also know that God created everything that is, from nothing, so that has to mean he created time, too. Einstein showed us that time is part of material reality, and since all of that is created by God, what sense does it make that there was capital-N nothing but somewhere deep in that nothing, a clock was ticking? Nothing is not nothing if it is subject to time. Time did not precede God, he created it. We should not imagine that once he created it, he subordinated himself to it or was overpowered by it. It makes no sense that he created and stands behind all of material reality as it unfolds in a particular time direction, but doesn't know where it's going.

What does make sense is that God stands outside of time, so he looks in on our lives from the outside, so to speak. It makes sense that he can see everything that is going on in our lives now and in the future because all moments are before him continuously. Again our language is unhelpful to trying to perceive as God does: "continuously" is another time-bound word. We could say he sees all events "simultaneously," but that's also a time-bound word, and therefore also not quite right. If he observes from outside of time, there's also not a moment during which he does the observing.

God is bigger than all this. In fact, this rumination on the nature of predestination and free will is helpful if for no other reason than as an aid to understanding just how fundamental is the difference between us and God. It is difficult for us to even conceive a physical reality without time as one of its boundaries, but clearly God can. Whether something happens in the future or not is a time-bound question, and God is not time-bound like we are. Only for human beings is there tension between free will and predestination.

It's a good idea in general to get out of the habit of thinking of God as if he were kind of a super-hero. That's a mistake often made by people who are looking for an avenue of escape from what they've come to consider a Christian bubble, especially the cloying bubble of Christianity practiced Protestant southern-American style. It's easy to throw over one's last allegiance to a putative God if we take him to be a limited pagan demiurge: idiosyncratic, petulant, and comical. But if he's not those things, if he's the Lord of the universe, then we need to stop thinking of him as if he were like us only maybe super-smart.

If there is no God, and mankind has its origins solely in evolutionary biological development, what does that portend for this question whether our lives and the endings of our lives are preordained in some way? We would have a more significant kind of predestination, one that is deadly to our self-image as human beings. Freedom disappears. Free will disappears. Agency disappears. If there is no God, and all of reality is material or a derived property of that which is material, then there is a kind of predestination for all of human events, but "predestination" is not the precise word because there is no One to predestine. Instead, events are predetermined: at the beginning of all physical things, matter was set in motion in such a way that all future events inexorably unfold as they must based on that first state of matter. There was no Mind at the Big Bang to preconceive today's graceful winged lift of the butterfly on the bush outside my window, but all the material parts of the butterfly and its environment came into existence then, and began the trajectory into space and into stardust and into the earth and the coalescing of the elements to sustain life and advances by evolution from inorganic particles to butterflies, including specifically this one at this moment at this place.

CHAPTER 8: HISTORY

As for the butterfly, so for human beings, in every action and thought of our lives. We don't have freedom, in the materialist paradigm, because our actions and thoughts were determined at the Big Bang. Nor do we have moral freedom, the ability to choose evil or to choose good. But neither do we have moral responsibility. It feels like we choose this course of action and reject another, but it is all an illusion.

Chapter 9: **Desire for Freedom**

Personal autonomy

THE INESCAPABLE DESIRE WE all have for freedom is important evidence to be evaluated. "Freedom" is almost always regarded as a positive good, but it is a word so ill-defined, absent context, as to potentially create mischief. For example, "America" and "freedom" are presented to American ears as being almost synonymous. In our political history, the colonies declared their independence from England, and then made that declaration a reality through armed revolution. So American colonies secured "freedom" from England. That certainly didn't mean, however, that individual Americans were free from privation and want, or from death or disability, or even from the constraints of the more local governments which supplanted England's.

In economic theory, we speak frequently of "freedom" as meaning individual choice in consumer purchases, and unconstrained movement of capital and trade, usually with the connotation that the absence of constraint positively serves human needs and desires. But every discussion of economic freedom really begins and ends with its opposite: scarcity. What we need and want is not available in unlimited supply, nor at zero cost. Economic freedom means only unrestrained trade, not freedom from want.

Both the political and economic ideas of "freedom" presuppose some forms of restraint. We have freedom in the sense of having the ability to participate in the making of laws and selection of law-makers, but we're all constrained by the outcome of the political process, whether we like it or not. We have freedom in the sense of being able to spend our money on what we want, but our choices are not infinite and neither is our money. We all make economic decisions within the constraints of our personal budgets and the market's offerings. This may seem obvious, but the point here is that our freedom politically and economically is not absolute. Constraints on our freedom are unalterable facts of life.

CHAPTER 9: DESIRE FOR FREEDOM

So it is with moral freedom, or "freedom of conscience." We all desire freedom to decide for ourselves what is right and wrong. To a certain extent we have it, but it is not absolute. None of us really thinks that our freedom should be so absolute as to justify, to pick an extreme example, freedom to murder another person. Others have freedom, too, and their freedom most fundamentally includes the freedom to go on living. Compromises to our personal freedoms are inevitable throughout all of society and all of history. It has ever been so. And yet, this most obvious of things must be said, because our culture includes a fuzzy misguided idea of absolute personal autonomy that may be at odds with human thriving. There is a tendency, at least in America in the early twenty-first century, to feel ourselves entitled to a radical individualism that tells us we can do and have and be whatever we want.

We acknowledge the boundaries to that radical autonomy as being harm to other people, but then, to reduce even that boundary, we tend to downplay that harm. Our culture tells us that others must acquiesce to our bending of reality to suit ourselves. We're really not acting individually without impact on the larger society around us. Personal autonomy is played out as insisting on change in society to make our personal choices more acceptable, not counting the infringement on others' autonomy, in doing so. We tend to operate on the continual fiction that the choices we make are only personal and individual, when they manifestly are not. In this way we seem to place a high value on personal autonomy as a form of freedom. But then the exercise of personal autonomy must be accommodated by society at large, and so that impacts the freedom of the other individuals within it.

Agency

We can describe freedom beyond the overly simplistic idea of personal autonomy as agency. We think of the word "agency" as representation of another in some capacity, such as a lawyer or real estate agent or insurance broker or someone to whom you give power of attorney. In such situations the person acquires "agency" for you, because you grant them power to effectuate your will, usually in some particular prescribed matter. The agency originates with you, however. "Agency" means freedom and power to act for oneself. We use the word "agency" to describe circumstances in which it is legally delegated, but the primary meaning is one's own self-directed exercise of will. The word is used in philosophy to denote real moral choice on the part of individuals, rather than deterministic or predestined conduct which is the result of illusory decision-making.

Individual moral freedom is at the heart of our criminal justice system. People can be punished for violating minimal moral standards codified in the law because we ascribe to people moral responsibility for what they do—it is an incident of their freedom. We don't put animals in jail if they do something we don't like, because they don't have the same moral responsibility. People go to jail because we hold them responsible for what they do, and we hold them responsible because we honor their freedom in moral decision-making.

The idea that a person has freedom and power to self-direct their conduct has not been universal, historically. In societies highly stratified by class, lower classes have less agency because more of their conduct and therefore more of their thought-lives are directed to effectuating the will of others. A chattel slave is quintessentially one who has minimal agency, having instead only freedom and power to act on the will of the master. This is the primary reason, in fact, that we disapprove slavery. We prize individual agency because we regard agency as fundamental to our humanity. Among the reasons why slavery is abhorrent is that we hold slaves responsible for their conduct, too, despite their dehumanizing conditions. Moral responsibility is an ineradicable feature of their humanity, just as it is for their slavemasters. The solution to their problem of stunted agency is to free them, not to absolve them from moral responsibility as we do animals, thereby further dehumanizing them.

Why? It is because people are or should be self-sovereign, choosing for themselves what they will do. Their actions are not prescribed by deities or by the deterministic unfolding of contingent causes and events. We say people have *free will*, and so we're sharply critical of social, cultural, or political impingements on the exercise of free will. Free will exercised politically implies self-governance. Self-governance, free will, and individual autonomy rest upon the idea of agency, and they are high values in liberal (classically liberal) societies. "Liberalism" refers to liberation from restrictions on individual agency.

If liberalism means greater recognition of human agency in the form of self-governance, free will, and individual autonomy, does that mean greater liberalism is always better? Yes, but we have to look carefully at whether particular social and cultural and political movements actually liberate, or

CHAPTER 9: DESIRE FOR FREEDOM

have the opposite effect practically. We want to advance this liberal value but be tempered in how we do it because of our recognition of the disorder in the world. Well-meaning movements to advance individual autonomy often paradoxically repose more power in the State or in a coercive cultural consensus, thus undermining the move to liberalism, resulting, in fact, in illiberalism—a return to diminished personal agency.

Where do we get the idea of agency, if it has not always been a given in our outlook? In the pagan world, much of what happened to people was thought to be caused by the gods or by "fate," a destiny vaguely attributed to causes outside the control of human beings. Among the Jews, however, a different outlook prevailed: a belief that God made man with free will, and that because mankind was extremely important to God, it very much mattered to God how people exercised that free will. Christians were admonished by Jesus and later theologians making sense of his Advent to self-govern with a recognition that there are consequences to individual choices. Unity with God, in the person of Christ, enabled people to choose well. A fatalistic way of thinking was to be overthrown in favor of recognizing one's agency, the view subjectively that one's personal decisions are eternally consequential.

Although largely materialist secular society retains the idea of agency, it would cut off the source of it. We think of human beings as having agency because of the Judaeo-Christian antecedents for the idea, but where does that leave us if we cast off the religious view of reality that gave rise to it? The concept of agency must diminish. If our conscience is derived from evolution and not placed in us by God, where does that leave us?

For one thing, the very idea of agency should be suspect, if we are to be consistent. Why are we individually responsible for the consequences of violating the conscience, and to whom are we responsible? The only answer, in the materialist paradigm, is that society evolves its moral code, and authority lies with contemporary society itself. But society enjoys no more authority for its moral values, than does an individual within it. Society tells us what is right and wrong, and it is codified in our laws and cultural influences, but because there is no independent, objective source for that moral code, it will change as society does. Adherence to the tribal code is the sole source of right and wrong; society and not God has ultimate moral authority. One would expect enforcement of rigid moral conformity, in such an environment, and that is what is happening. Individual moral agency escheats to the collective and we think that seems proper because we envision it originating in the collective, both in our collective past, expressed in our DNA, and in our present, expressed in politically correct tribal thinking.

Time Horizon

Philosophers and physicists and theologians struggle mightily with the concept of time. It is among the things which seem hard-wired into us, as with the unalterable base-line orientation we have to truth and beauty and the pull of conscience. It is nearly inconceivable that we might exist outside of time, or that time might flow in the opposite or multiple directions, or that it would proceed unevenly, in fits and starts. But why not?

That space and time are connected is quite intriguing. Suddenly time is much more elastic than we imagined. If we traveled in space, really fast, we might age more slowly than our contemporaries back on earth! Theoretically possible. Time needn't run smoothly in an uninterrupted way, as we perceive it doing day-to-day. It can be modified in the same way as can physical things measured spatially, at least theoretically.

We hinted at the idea that heaven might be characterized as timelessness, or that in any event God might be One who is timeless, while all of us inside of his creation are burdened with the perception of a time-restraint. We can think of time and space as restraints rather than merely features of our current reality. It could be that the hallmark of supernatural reality is the removal of those constraints. Thinking in this way could be helpful to us in understanding how to thrive in this life.

To do so, let's consider the subjective sense of time that we each have. Not in the sense that "time flies," or "I can't believe it's already August," or that kind of thing. Rather, the way we think of our lives lived as a whole. We all know we're going to die, and yet in our daily life we think of this project or that event or general plans for the future as if we're going to live forever. We can lapse into thinking that what we do doesn't matter in the long run. But of course, there is no "long run," really. We die. There is an ongoing tension in each of us, between living as if there is no tomorrow, and as if our tomorrows will stretch into eternity. This internal psychological tension is sometimes described in terms of a "time horizon." It is the degree to which we can subjectively project our future. It is the degree to which, at this moment, a person can place his present thoughts and actions in a continuum stretching into the finite future.

CHAPTER 9: DESIRE FOR FREEDOM

Let's say you're twenty-five years old. God willing, most of your life is ahead of you. It mostly hasn't happened yet. It's more difficult to sustain a long time horizon, because so much of life to this point has been contingent—occurring this way and not that because of things you don't control. At twenty-five it's relatively hard to correlate today's actions to your state of being tomorrow. The farther away that "tomorrow," the harder it is to imagine. You can picture life at twenty-six, but it's much harder to picture life at forty. Too many variables, between now and then, and that's assuming you live that long. So while you might connect your actions today to their consequences next year, fifteen years out may be beyond your imagination's range. It might as well be another lifetime, happening to someone else. Your time horizon at twenty-five, you would say, is somewhere short of fifteen years.

Now imagine what the time horizon might be for someone who is sixty. That person's time horizon might well extend beyond the date of his own death. He is likely to have greater concern for his legacy, and a heightened sense of urgency about what he does with his life because of thoughts of his mortality and the big question of what comes next. A person whose time horizon has stretched in this way begins to see his life lived as a whole, such that he's not concerned only with the past that has already happened and cannot be changed, but also with the future, all of which is now inside his time horizon. He can think of his life as a whole; as a completed story, now boxed up and accessible to understanding from the outside. What is he to make of the content of the box in its entirety?

A person thinking this way has achieved a high degree of maturity. Obviously, many sixty-year-olds haven't actually achieved it, and some twenty-five-year-olds have. But it's a helpful way of thinking about time and the moral sense we all have.

Misbehavior is often the result of a short time horizon. Not that a short time horizon is the only reason for immoral behavior, but a person who can't see beyond the immediate future is much more likely to live from impulse to impulse, without ability to sublimate them, respond properly to them, and tie their actions into a larger narrative of a life well-lived. We all know of people who live with no wider view of meaning or purpose—passive, hapless people often in trouble and addictions and self-induced oppressions, for whom life is nothing more than a meaningless series of one darned inexplicable thing after another.

If our time horizon is very short, then our life is in a sense not a life at all, but a series of lived snippets of time. We're conscious; we're aware; we follow by logical inference the consequences of our acts, but only within a short range of time.

If our time horizon is long, then our life makes sense as a whole; everything we do is tied to everything else, even though there are variables we don't control. Indeed, the uncontrollable variables become fewer, because with a longer view of life in mind, many turn out not to be so uncontrollable after all. Our life as a whole begins to make more sense, if our time horizon is long. Our time horizon expands toward the length of our actual life, and can expand beyond, too. Expanded in this way, it approaches a perspective of timelessness. We can thus approach the freedom of heaven even in this life.

Chapter 10: **Conscience**

What is Morality

A KEY BIT OF evidence on the ultimate question of God's existence is the conscience. Everyone has a conscience, regardless of their beliefs about the scope of metaphysical reality. Atheists have a conscience. Christians do. Buddhists, Muslims—everyone. Where does it come from, and what does its existence and content tell us?

Our conscience answers for us whether some act or omission is moral or immoral. Morality is a sensitive subject because of associations people make with the word. It is sometimes associated with professing Christian faith, hence the criticism of hypocrisy by skeptics, when they see immoral conduct by Christians. The word (morality) has sometimes been used to refer not to right and wrong in general, but to sexual morality in particular. This adds another layer of sensitivity, given changing sexual mores in the last two generations. And of course, everyone is sensitive to the suggestion, made subtly or overtly, that another person is their moral better.

Because people approach the topic of morality with heightened caution, it is especially important to be clear about what it means. To start with, consider "morality" to be a value-neutral word. It might seem, superficially, that this word of all words cannot be considered value-neutral, but it is, really. "Morality" denotes a subject matter, not a quantum of goodness. If we consider the source of morality, for example, we consider why it is that people consider some conduct good, and some bad. To have a coherent discussion of how we come to think of things as moral or immoral, we have to be able to speak of good and bad conceptually, rather than simply whether a particular act is good or bad.

To understand morality conceptually, consider truth by way of analogy. We routinely say this thing is true; this other thing is false. We understand this to be a proper application of the idea of "truth," but there is a more abstract conceptual level for truth, too. We consider truth in the abstract when we think about where truth comes from, and why we are oriented to make truth and falsity distinctions in every waking moment.

Likewise with morality. We routinely think of this act or that omission as being immoral, or displays of virtue as moral, but we can think of morality on a conceptual level too. That is, we can consider where morality comes from and why we are discerning about it and why we make judgments of other people on the basis of it, without undertaking to classify a particular act as moral or immoral.

Desirable vs. Moral

What makes one act good, and another bad? Why do we ascribe a morality component to a particular act or omission, rather than just noting it as desirable or undesirable? Why do we think of others' acts or omissions in moral terms even when they don't affect us? Why do we consider an act not only undesirable, but opprobrious? Why do we add to some undesirable acts a feeling of human corruption, as well? Why do we attach moral significance to things people do, but not to things animals do, or to things that happen naturally without human cause? Why do we adjust our feelings about another person on the basis of their conduct? Why do we judge?

Morality is one of those things hard-wired into us, so much so that we have a hard time defining it without using the word in the definition. To even define morality, we end up using near-synonyms, like "virtue," or phrases like "right and wrong" which assume the very thing we're trying to describe, and leave out the feelings of shame and honor that also attach to moral rightness and wrongness of human actions.

It is often said that non-material aspirations of mankind devolve to these three: the good, the true, and the beautiful. Much that is aspirational in human beings can be described with greater specificity than these three broad categories, but these three seem to be the irreducible elements of aspirational, non-material, and idealistic visions of humanity. All three of these elements are instinctive and basic in our humanity. They provide orientation to all our thoughts and actions. We may deviate from that which is good, or true, or beautiful, but even in doing so we implicitly acknowledge the true north from which we deviate. Even in the act of lying, we acknowledge the orientation to truth. That's why we can call a lie a lie. Even in the face of ugliness, we acknowledge our orientation to that which is beautiful. That's why we recognize ugliness for what it is. And even when we engage in immoral conduct, we harbor feelings of shame or regret because we are fundamentally oriented according to moral good and evil.

Not only are these baseline orientations for individuals, they are consistent across society as well; that is, we all hold these orientations in common. They are universals. We all seek the good, the true, and the beautiful, and we all are aware that we all do. They are collective, as well as individual, orientations. Whatever else one might say about morality, there is no denying its prominence in our day-to-day experience. It is the controlling plot element in every book, movie or play we will ever see. It is among the primary animating influences on us all day, every day. It is basic like our desires for companionship, love, food, and shelter.

Despite all this, it is possible to go through life not really conscious of the role our sense of morality plays in how we live. It is possible to formulate one's sense of right and wrong by defaulting to what society around us sets as minimally acceptable behavior. Likewise we may come to admire as virtuous what society identifies for us as virtuous, without delving deeper into what makes it so. It may be that we purposely shape the dictates of our conscience to conform to what the society around us tells us it should be. But social mores change over time, and are different from place to place. We should consider whether that means morality is an ever-changing thing, specific to a particular time and place, or whether it is something universal across time and people-groups.

Source according to Theism

According to Judaism and Christianity, human beings are made in the image of God. What does it mean that we are made in his "image," given that he is immaterial? There are several aspects of humanity that point to our being his image-bearers, but perhaps most obviously it is morality.

How curious that we would attach a moral rightness or wrongness to anything we do. It gives our actions a significance they wouldn't otherwise have. If we lived according to instinct, as animals do, there would be no reason to call our actions morally "good" or "bad." They might be good or bad in the sense of being merely desirable or undesirable, but that is a good and bad untethered to moral imperative.

A funny video in yesterday's news feed had an ant scrabbling across a table-top with a tiny loose diamond. Apparently this occurred atop a jeweler's bench. The ant pulled off the heist and was making his get-away with the diamond, for whatever reason ants lug tiny stones around. The caper was a bad thing as far as the jeweler was concerned—or would have been if the ant had gotten away with it—but no one called the ant-police to come bring the ant to justice.

To illustrate the depths of evil in the world, people sometimes refer to the intentional bombing of the Oklahoma City federal building in 1995. It was horrible because of the loss of life, but it was all the worse that a human being caused all this destruction. He had what the law might describe as a "malignant heart." But suppose the same toll had resulted from mice nibbling wires, causing a fire? The tragic loss would be no different, but we would hardly say it was an issue of morality, any more than we find moral fault with the diamond-toting ant.

Human beings are different from everything else in the material world. We are responsible, morally, for what we do and fail to do. Our entire criminal justice system is premised on the idea that we are morally responsible. We are deemed to have agency: autonomy in our moral decision-making. It is for this reason that we are answerable to society's moral code, codified in the criminal law. Individually, we feel intensely the departures from what we know to be right morally. We're prone to feel regret at moral wrong, perhaps to the point of committing to henceforth doing right, and to rectifying as far as we can the consequences of our moral error; i.e., repentance.

Our grasp of morality is internalized in the conscience. We can of course ignore that internal voice, but doing so requires a purposeful tamping down of our moral awareness, perhaps by self-delusion, or just by intentional repudiation of what we know to be right in favor of something we want more than a clear conscience. Or if the criminal law and cultural mores are sufficiently loose compared to our internal voice of conscience, we may throw-over active moral judgment and lazily default to the minimal requirements of the society around us.

We bear within us an orientation to the good, and deviations from that register as an internal voice in our consciousness in a negative way. We may say in such an instance that our moral compass has gone awry. Everyone has a conscience, it is not unique to Christians, certainly. We feel guilt, when we ignore our conscience, at least until we habituate ourselves to it so that the internal voice is quieted almost to silence. Through an accumulation of this kind of tamping-down we can develop a rough interior, so to speak, becoming relatively more immune to the dictates of conscience as we go.

CHAPTER 10: CONSCIENCE

The conscience comes from God. He is the author of all good, and he placed his law on our hearts. The Bible suggests mankind's unity with God in that mankind has, as a pale reflection of God, moral awareness and moral freedom. God gave mankind the capacity to embrace good or evil. Ultimate good is God. Mankind was given the capacity to accept or reject God, so that we could have genuine and unforced love for God. That moral freedom can also be exercised to reject God, however. Through disloyalty to God, in acts of attempted self-promotion to the status of a god, we become estranged from the true God. As a result we carry an intense awareness of our separation from him. We can turn and accept his reconciliation to us, or we can try on our own to manage the damage as best we can despite having broken the world.

Source according to Materialism

The fact of moral thinking is evidence to be explained. If theism is false, where does morality come from? There being no God to do the creating of mankind with a conscience, the best alternative explanation on offer is naturalistic evolution. The idea would be that mankind developed passively through an evolutionary process that commenced with inorganic matter. This is true of his biology, including his brain, and his brain is the repository of certain immaterial features which emerge from the physical brain, including consciousness.

Morality, on this view, is an evolved phenomenon. As with any evolved phenomenon, it exists because it enhances survival, and therefore persisted and further developed in successive generations of people. It did so because the moral sense enhanced social living, which in turn enhanced survivability. The way this would work is that in a particular population, some individuals would be more cooperative with other individuals, and some less so. Those that were more cooperative were more likely to survive. As a result, in successive generations the population would be composed of progressively more socially cooperative individuals. That tendency to social cooperation manifested, over time, feelings of empathy which underlie much of what we recognize now as morally right conduct. Thus, the "Golden Rule" (do unto others as you would have them do unto you) is thought to be a biological codification of evolved tendencies.

By this theory, the dictates of our conscience are not the result of objective good and bad, but instincts of good and bad resulting from the evolutionary process. It means the conscience is based on what has in the past been helpful and unhelpful to survival, not on what is objectively morally good or bad. Superficially, that may sound like a distinction without a difference, because the conscience is the conscience, regardless whether it is God-given or evolved. It does matter, however, because of the question of *authority*. The significance can be discerned by asking this important question: by what authority should a person do or refrain from doing something?

The answer is obvious, if morality comes from God. God's decrees are unchanging and applicable to everyone, and we are aware of them through our conscience. Moral failings have consequences. But if conscience is a hard-wired intuition resulting from our evolved biology, then it is instinct only, and has no more authority over what we actually do than does our reason or our present desires. To express this in stark terms, if reason tells us we can get away with murder, the reasoned calculation might green-light Raskolnikov's enterprise, overcoming the hesitation of conscience. If my conscience is biological instinct only, that source of authority, such as it is, is easily overcome by another source of authority, such as my reason. My reason is guided not by instinct, but by self-interest, including social approbation or opprobrium associated with situational ethics, and relativistic considerations, such as how the deviations from instinct I am considering compare to others'. If society as a whole is declining morally, then reason might take me to the conclusion that my conduct is adequate if it is no worse than the current standards of society.

Moreover, my conscience is easily overcome, if it is understood as being only the product of evolved intuition. If the society around me tells me that my moral instincts are outmoded or superseded, why wouldn't I regard those messages as being just as authoritative as my evolved intuition? There would be no reason; in fact it is easily justified by the supposition that my evolved instincts are shaped by social living, and the current deviations from my instincts—my conscience—are also shaped by social living. This means least-common-denominator living. If society around me says it's ok, it's ok. There would be no individual brake on society-wide moral decline, if the materialist explanation for conscience were true.

Another difficulty with the materialist theory for the origin of morality is that it simply leaves out some of the human motivations that inhere in the conscience, that could not possibly come from evolution premised on social living. The human conscience includes elements of humility,

CHAPTER 10: CONSCIENCE

thankfulness, and reverence, for example, that are inexplicable as being necessary to social living. Perhaps some form of humility translates to agreeableness, which makes us easier to live with, so that humility could become a part of our DNA. But not the genuine humility that goes with the sense that there is something greater than mankind.

Our conscience also tells us we should be thankful, but why, if that part of our intuition is purely evolved? We might be thankful to other people, if they help us or give us something—that again would be part of a general evolved strategy of agreeableness—but it doesn't explain the general sense of thankfulness for life or prosperity independent of thankfulness to other people, such as we feel most explicitly on occasions like Thanksgiving, where the gratitude is explicitly directed beyond society presently or in times past. And that instinct for gratitude based on humility has yet another dimension, which we refer to as reverence, distinct from humility and gratitude and explicitly directed to something greater than people or the society of people.

To be sure, there are theories of religion's origins which would attempt to explain how religious motivations are hard-wired into us though religious doctrines are false. For example, there is the theory that religion itself evolved from the needs of social living, such that we achieve tribal solidarity by all of us together believing in an authority outside the tribe. The idea would be that over large amounts of time, the outward-looking turn to deities or to common spirituality becomes itself hard-wired in the DNA of successive generations, so that, one could argue, that outward-look, as with gratitude and reverence, itself becomes part of one's evolved moral instinct.

This is a lot of evolutionary weight to put on the necessity of social living, however, and it has the effect of trivializing reason and evidence in the adoption of religious belief. It certainly doesn't enhance social living or survival to be martyred for one's faith. Early Christians were ostracized by society; their conscience did not lead them away from their religious beliefs as it should have, on this theory. The history of the Jews is one long story of following God-ordained conscience rather than assimilate with neighboring tribes, often at great cost, humanly-speaking.

The evolutionary theory for conscience leaves out another important element, which is that even if evolution accounted for the instinct for or against a particular course of action, it would not explain the "rightness" or "wrongness" of it. Suppose for example we instinctively respect our neighbor's property because our evolution-derived impulses thus compel us.

Authoritativeness for that instinct is missing. It's one thing to want to do the right thing; it's quite another to explain why it's "right."

Moreover, these two things are contradictory. If we exhibit traits that we collectively regard as ethical because those traits are naturally selected for, then there is no basis for saying we *ought* to exhibit those traits. They exist, according to the theory, in the same way as do physical traits like height or eye color. At the same time, if those traits are authoritative, then they cannot be mere products of evolution. Materialists have to be saying both that: (a) morality is a contingent product of brute, amoral nature, and (b) that morality is binding upon the conscience of rational man. That is a contradiction.

Morality as explained by theists requires no such contradiction. For theists, good is an eternal reality, a transcendent truth that is of the very essence of God. God is not merely a superlatively good contingent being, but the ontological substance of goodness. God is good, not only in the sense that He does good, but in the sense that He is goodness itself.

If our moral sense (and for that matter, all our intuitions, as with our intuited *sensus divinitatus*) developed through evolution, that would mean all that evolved information content exists physically in our brains at birth. So that means it is impossible that we are born a *tabula rasa*, to be imprinted by our environments including our social environment. So where is the warrant for socially-derived modification to our moral sense? Why would society now say, for example, that sex outside marriage is ok, when two generations ago (too recent for evolutionary change) it was not? Racism is decried almost universally, now, but quite recently in evolutionary terms, it was acceptable. Clearly, this moral relaxation (in the case of sexual rectitude) and moral refinement (in the case of anti-racism) are not derived from evolution, but from some other source.

Theists already have an answer for this, of course: it is that we have an unchanging moral code imprinted on our hearts, and it has a transcendent source which is itself timeless and unchanging. Changes in social mores can only be changes toward or away from that unwavering standard.

Materialists would have to have conflicting answers, leaving them with an ineradicable dissonance. On the one hand, our moral code is the result of evolution. On the other hand, moral arguments are made regularly that are clearly independent of that evolution. It seems clear that removing the transcendent source leaves us with a battleground, socially, for what is to be considered moral and immoral, but why, if the source of morality is hard-wired by evolution?

Some materialists go a step further, and use man's evolved social traits as an explanation for religion, too. A fairly popular explanation of the prevalence of religion is that it is a way of institutionalizing that social adaptation. Religions themselves evolve, the theory goes, as a means of cementing the social mores necessary for communal living. Religious doctrine is not true, on this theory, but it is socially useful. We want to feel we're a part of something important. This belief about religion has long had traction, and finds its articulation in works like Emile Durkheim's *The Elementary Forms of Religious Life* (1912).

A pragmatic atheist might accept the fact of religions as useful to society and as a natural result of evolution, but would hold their doctrines simply not true. But those who subscribe to a naturalist worldview must account for morality without using religion as a crutch. If materialism is a correct understanding of reality, then matter came from absolute nothing; life came from non-life; human consciousness came from animal consciousness; and morality came from evolution of man in the same way that walking upright is thought to have done. Materialism necessarily holds that our brains are hard-wired with the Golden Rule through a process of biological variation meeting environmental challenge. The life form that became man exists as it does because the long, long process of passive genetic deselection left individuals with a predisposition to defer to communal values.

Thus, we have two competing claims for the source of conscience. A top-down view, that it is implanted in us by God; and a bottom-up view, that it originates with the unguided movement of matter over time and culminates in a highly complex being with an internal directedness to that which he calls "good."

Humanism

Always and everywhere, there is a sense that human beings are special among other living things. No one thinks twice about cutting back vegetation or killing an animal to eat, but killing a person is heinous, instantly recognizable to anyone as the gravest of wrongs one can commit; the deepest depth of immoral conduct.

Why?

The materialist view and the theist view can be succinctly stated. For theists, it's a matter of being made in the image of God—special from the moment of man's creation. For those who reject a Creator-imputed specialness, and embrace unguided naturalistic evolution as the sole explanation for the provenance of mankind, the answer is survival, pure and simple. Man must eat to survive, and any moral compunctions about what is eaten must be overcome, to survive. The need to eat living things stops (usually) with other people, because social living also enhances survival.

Let's first consider what does not explain human specialness. If you begin to research the question of what makes people special as compared to animals, you will probably first find explanations of features of human beings that are unique, like high intelligence, big brains, speech-making ability, opposable thumbs, social cooperation, and the like. Materialist explanations devolve to the proposition that mankind is superior to other animals because of accidents of evolution. But that doesn't get at why mankind is special. It just explains why man dominates over other animals, if naturalistic evolution is true. Our question is different. Why do we think that harm to other people has moral implications that harm to other living things doesn't? The question isn't why humans are superior physically. The question is why we regard them as morally different in kind than all other living things.

Materialists struggle for an explanation of the special-ness of human beings that does not depend on their being made in the image of God; as moral agents in their own right, able to choose between good and evil. Sometimes the discussion centers on truly distinctive elements of humanity, such as shared cultural memory, the principle that we each of us carry around a trove of understanding, historical and present, of the mutual expectations of person to person in society. That is still merely a distinctive, however, it is not an explanation for why the distinction sets mankind apart morally from other living things.

Another explanation sometimes made is that human beings have a kind of mutual regard which elevates us each in the eyes of others. That mutual regard results from a feature of human consciousness, wherein our sense of self-awareness is much more developed than an animal's in that we carry about a mental image of ourselves as through the eyes of others. Each encounter is therefore a subject-to-subject encounter. This would explain why a human would regard another human as special. I'm special and you're a human, too, so you're also special. But even this is just a distinctive of humans as compared to other animals; another reason why we might consider ourselves superior among animals. It is not a reason why humans exist on a moral plane that animals do not inhabit.

Humans are the only animals with complex speech, shared cultural memory, consciousness as described here, depth of emotion, complex social living, and so on. But that's not what makes humans special. Humans are also the only species that judges and imprisons members of the species. That may sound like a negative, but it highlights a positive: humans are the only animals that embrace a full range of moral accountability, and link that moral accountability to moral freedom, and thence to actual freedom, and thence to liberation as a form of individual flourishing. These are elements of morality that exist and indeed can only exist because our moral sense comes from our awareness of God, who places the moral code on our hearts and reveals it to us explicitly.

Morality and Time

Is there a connection between morality and our experience of the physical restraint of time? We live our life in a time-linear way. We start at a definite point, we move forward in a straight "line," and we end at a definite point. At the moment that is "now," our understanding is well-illuminated. The line behind "now" is in our memory, and the farther back we imagine, the dimmer it is. There's a reason we sometimes don't learn from our mistakes. The line ahead of "now" is unknown, except insofar as we can extrapolate from our current trajectory.

Imagine that same life lived outside of time. Imagine that instead of living incrementally constrained to this line with a dim picture of past and future, the moments of your life are contained loose in a box, and not only that, but you stand on the outside of it, looking in, seeing all the moments at once. You have a big box of "now's."

Perhaps this is God's perspective. If you were outside the box of your life, you would arrange all your "now's" into a coherent whole. You would give those "now's" a place in a story which has purpose and meaning. You wouldn't make a hash of any of those "now's." You'd live well. In fact, you'd live perfectly. You'd live a morally perfect life.

Is this what it means to live in eternity? Is this box-perspective the more real perspective, as compared to the life we live this side of the veil? Maybe all of this life in the body is just a march we're given to undertake with limited perspective, in which God is engaged in trying to stretch our time horizons, like he did with the Israelites, readying us for eternity. We march with trust that when we reach eternity, that wider perspective will become ours. We trust that there is not just more than this life, but there's a whole new set of dimensions, an expansive view of reality that cannot be perceived now. It is as though now we look through a glass but darkly (that is, in a dim mirror with limited understanding of ourselves), but when we are with God we will see ourselves as if face-to-face;* on the outside, and in eternity, looking back on ourselves.

You might try reading the historical books of the Old Testament fast, not pausing to try to pick up this nuance or that one. You would see that it screams to us of the coming Christ, but you might see something else, too: Over and over again God's people were frustrated in their efforts to follow God because their time horizons were too short. Over and over again God reconciled them to himself by re-invigorating their temporal perspectives. The entire Old Testament is one long stretching of the time horizons of God's people.

The Bible is also of course about right conduct. Might these be connected? Right moral conduct; right understanding of time. We may not understand eternity fully, yet, but we can stretch our time horizons to understand it better, and we can understand the connection between that expanded time horizon and living a better, fuller, more meaningful life, with fewer regrets and with more richness. Or as described in the Bible: "abundantly."

If there is no God there is no eternal life, and following our human death there is only oblivion. Everything in existence, in this view, is time-bound. Timelessness is only a thought experiment, it has no counterpart in reality, for someone who buys into the materialist paradigm. From that perspective, the sense of right and wrong we have, and the kinds of conduct we describe as "moral" and "immoral," are not a function of timelessness, but are a function of time, instead. Eons of time are said to result in evolution of both the sense of right and wrong, and the specific behaviors we attach those labels to.

We would all do well to better understand the theory behind the non-teleological, biological evolution of naturalism. Understanding is sometimes made difficult because so often the explanations sneak in a teleology that is supposedly absent. Discussions of evolution seem always to include

---

*1 Corinthians 13:12.

CHAPTER 10: CONSCIENCE

some notion of purpose or directedness inhering in the genes. We're to imagine individuals and populations *wanting* something. That means individuals and populations have an object of desire, which gives them purpose. They direct their will toward that purpose. If we suppose that the individual genes of our body have a will and a direction and a purpose, we're giving credence to our intuition that there is an external and transcendent source for that will and direction and purpose.

This is not to say that evolution is a false theory, necessarily, but it does mean we should be careful with how much we think it explains. The theory of evolution is usually understood to encompass a materialist paradigm for reality. Evolution on this understanding holds there is no driver of biological development at all. It is utterly passive; it is not *driven* by anything. The passage of eons of time is sometimes confused as being the "driver" of evolution, but that's not what the theory actually holds. In fact, the theory supposes vast amounts of time precisely because the process lacks an external driver such as design, direction, will, or purpose.

Naturalistic evolution imagines variation within a population, and the population subjected to environmental pressure, with the result that some combinations of variants survive, and others die. Though this is referred to as "adaptation," we have to remain mindful that no individuals actually adapt. A population doesn't either, except in the passive sense that the changed conditions result in a population with a different combination of genetic variations. To be accurate about naturalistic evolution, it would be better to use phrases like "results in," rather than "adapts" or "selects." Words and phrases like "natural selection" are misleading. The theory holds that no person or thing is doing any selecting. We just confusingly call it that. But when we call it that, we import notions of willfulness, purposefulness, and goal-directedness—all features which are supposedly excluded by a naturalistic version of evolution.

Materialists imagine that our beliefs about what is right and wrong, and our moral sense in general, are among the features of our existence derived from changes in genetic variation of human populations over time. Those with a heightened sense of empathy and mutual reciprocity survive; those without die. The population of humans acquires a shared social sensibility. In the materialist explanation of morality, our sense that particular behaviors are "right" or "wrong," and our intuitive moral sense in general, are based entirely on what was helpful to our evolving biology. Something is "good" not because it derives from some objective criterion, but only because our genes tell us it is. Something is "bad" not because it is associated with heedless, short-time-horizon thinking by one with moral agency, but because our genetic make-up makes it seem so.

This means we're genetically disposed to think of some behavior as carrying the label "moral good," or "moral bad;" the behaviors are not inherently so. Our conception of moral good and moral bad is necessarily an illusion. There's no such thing, in the naturalism paradigm. Indeed, on this understanding, evolution has programmed us to believe something inconsistent with the theory itself: that morality exists independent of our genetic make-up.

Moreover, it's not just that we're genetically programmed to regard some things as "good" and some as "bad." We're programmed to have a moral sense, so that we regard those "good" and "bad" things as *morally* good and bad. Our evolved genetic make-up (it is theorized) cause us to think of particular behaviors with moral approval, opprobrium, pride, or shame. We don't have moral agency because what seems to be moral decision-making is really just genetic predisposition to react to our environment in particular ways. There is only an evolved intuition to attach to those reactions the labels "good" or "bad."

Speaking in terms of morality is actually fundamentally wrong, if nature is all of reality. "Good" and "bad" and "moral" and "immoral" are words borrowed from a vocabulary that is meaningful only if morality has a transcendent source; if human beings have moral agency; if we are responsible for the things we do and fail to do. They only make sense if there is a moral Source outside the evolution of human existence.

From a materialist perspective that is consistent, "right" and "wrong" would be just labels attached to particular evolved intuitions. Why, if we adopt the materialist paradigm, do we nonetheless speak of "right" and "wrong?" And why would we ever argue about it? Presumably because of the always-present genetic variation within the population. So if I say abortion is wrong for everyone, and my neighbor says it's right for some, we're both responding to our programming. And, we can both be "right," because moral "rightness" doesn't really exist. Our respective intuitions could not involve an objective thing true for both of us, if naturalism correctly describes all of reality. One necessary result of this is a political power struggle as the sole means to resolve differences in moral judgment.

Chapter 11: **Truth and Rationality**

WE MIGHT HAVE A conversation in which we disagree on just about everything, and yet, without realizing it, agree on the most important thing. Suppose you insist there's a God, and I say there isn't. Or suppose we disagree on man-made global-warming. Perhaps you say it's true that man's activities materially contribute to climate change, and I say it's not true; that if climate change is occurring, it is not appreciably caused by human activity. We could go on like this, and find that we disagree on pretty much every subject. What you say is true, I say is untrue. What I say is true, you say is untrue. In all of that conversation, however, whether we realize it or not we're actually agreeing that truth is the criterion for the debate. It is the arbiter to which we both appeal. We may disagree on what is true, but we don't disagree that truth is what we seek. We share a truth orientation.

It is important to remember we're not talking here about whether something is true or not, but rather whether truth is what we both seek. If we were to disagree on the meta-principle, it might go like this. You might say it's true that we both seek truth. I might say it's not true that we both seek truth. But in doing so haven't we given away the game? We would merely be ratcheting the exchange up to another level of abstraction. We still seek truth.

The truth orientation is important evidence. Why do we have it? Is it ordained by God, or is it entirely evolved? Is it entirely a biological phenomenon; that is, a subjective experience of living things? Or is it something that exists in and through all physical things? Is truth ontological?

Source

The truth orientation is so much a part of the operating system of our lives that it's possible to never consider it. It's a bit like breathing. It's essential and yet we seldom think about it. Imagine that it didn't exist. There would be no rational ordering principle for the direction of our thoughts.

Thoughts would proceed randomly. Is there a lion in the bush waiting for me to walk by? We couldn't even ask the question, much less answer it in a way calculated to keep us alive. The truth orientation is so hard-wired that it is inconceivable there could be life without it.

But why? Where does it come from?

If naturalism explains reality, this feature of our mental processes like all other features of our physical being must be explained by non-teleological biological evolution. Seeking the truth of things (whether there's a lion in the bush) might make us more fit for survival. But this doesn't really answer the question. The issue isn't simply whether a truth orientation is more advantageous for us. The question is why are there objective features of our surroundings that lend themselves to being understood in binary terms like true/not-true. It's not just my mental processes that are at stake, when I detect or do not detect a lion in the bush. It's rather more important knowing—in binary terms—the truth or falsity of the lion-in-the-bush proposition.

We could say truth is itself ontological; that is, a necessary feature of existence. True objective features of our environment precede our perception of them. Is there or is there not a lion in the bush? The lion's very existence in that place is the subject of a binary yes/no truth determination. And my perception of the lion's presence is likewise the subject of my internal truth-detecting mental apparatus. Truth, we can say, is therefore bound up in the very fact of objective physical existence. At the first moment there is something rather than nothing, truth is spoken into the world.

Imagine there were no life. Would "truth" inhere in rocks and water and stars and galaxies? Those things must exist or not exist. It's a binary opposition, like an on/off light switch. If there is no existence, there is no truth attached to physical things, because there is absolute nothing. Actually, it doesn't quite fit to say "there is" absolute nothing, because "there is" announces existence. Better to say nothing physical exists, and so there can be no truth orientation in physical things.

But there are physical things. Moreover, there is clearly a truth orientation in some of those physical things; namely living things like people whose entire outlook is governed by discernment of truth and falsity. It is a subjective phenomenon in those living things, obviously, but truth can be said to inhere in the very existence of the things being observed. This would be necessary to the truth/falsity perception in the living things. Truth can be said to inhere in existing physical things that don't have subjective

CHAPTER 11: TRUTH AND RATIONALITY

experience, like rocks and air. Numerous mathematical constants are necessary to the existence or continued existence of those non-biological things, and certainly it is "true" that those constants exist, and that the information is proven true by the fact of existence, not just our perception of it. Physical things are imbued with informational content, in this way, and these mathematical "truths" point to the orientation of truth even apart from we human beings who are ourselves clearly oriented to truth.

There is an intriguing body of science developed over the last hundred years or so relating to quantum mechanics, which suggest paradoxes that ill-fit our historical Newtonian vision of physics, and may be explainable only by the ontological nature of truth. There is evidently physical reality that exists or not based on observation by truth-oriented sentient beings. Clearly that physical reality would have to have its own truth orientation, therefore, such that truth is indeed ontological. This is regarded by some as *The New Story of Science*, as suggested in a 1984 book with that title by Robert Augros and George Stanciu. Quantum mechanics point to truth being ontological; that is, inherent in the fact of physical existence. The better evidence is that the truth orientation is not merely a subjective feature of human consciousness. It is therefore an orientation of an active universal Mind that authors the cosmos.

Postmodernism

The meta-principle of truth orientation could be compromised, if we tinker with meanings to words. Suppose, in our imagined conversation, one of us says, "this conversation is not about truth." Well what does that mean? The statement is made in the conversation, so is it true, or not? We would quickly spiral out into an utterly meaningless exchange of words, in a fine display of postmodernist absurdity. This isn't idle wordplay, or a silly puzzle to think through. It's actually an example of how truth orientation is often a casualty in modern discourse.

You may experience this by being in a conversation in which an assertion you hear seems completely irrational. It can be frustrating, trying to figure out what is actually being said. It may be that you're working from a truth orientation, but you're having a conversation with someone who isn't. Postmodernism can be summarized as an attempt at abandonment of the truth orientation, in service to an argument which is in turn in service to an ideology. It is about advocacy, not finding the truth. It presupposes that "truth" is a human projection, to be developed rather than discovered.

Among other things, postmodernism presupposes there is no objective, "out there" truth. Rather, "truth," if used at all, is a label attached to the result of a process, and the process exists as an assertion of power. A power orientation takes the place of a truth orientation. With a truth orientation, the normal process is to reason to a conclusion. With a power orientation, this may be reversed, so that one may have a conclusion and then develop an argument to support it, and yet invoke "truth."

This would seem to obviously invite irrationality, but a person arguing outside the truth orientation may not be entirely irrational. That is, logical inferences build upon logical inferences for that person just like they do for someone speaking honestly from a truth orientation. But because the conclusion drives the process, rather than the process driving the conclusion, the person following the power orientation may hide away some inferences and build on unrevealed assumptions. If you listen to this from the standpoint of truth orientation, it makes no sense, and if you try to point out the logical flaws, you may find the expounder impervious to the criticism. You come to realize that logical reasoning is not the point. Advocacy is. It's not that a postmodernist can't think straight. It's that he doesn't want you to think straight.

It is common, in this world, for people to talk right past each other, because one operates with a truth orientation, and the other operates from a power orientation. Everyone operates from a truth orientation in their natural thinking processes. But people sometimes do not operate from that orientation in their advocacy. It's disingenuous, and we should be on guard against it. People who say there is no absolute truth are actually contending for an absolute truth: that there is no absolute truth. They appeal to the concept of truth in denying it exists. This approach is ubiquitous in this age, discernible once you begin to see it for what it is.

Rationality

Related to the truth orientation is the fact of rationality. Rationality is the logical progression of ideas, from observation to inference to conclusion. Rationality is related to the truth orientation because rationality involves a connectedness of linked thoughts, and that connectedness—logic—means one thought causes another, and another and another and so on. What

CHAPTER 11: TRUTH AND RATIONALITY

does "logical" mean? The word derives from "logos," which means "word;" specifically the word of God whereby truth is spoken into the world. Apart from the strictly religious sense, it implies semantic content; information. It is a pre-existing ordering criteria linking thought to thought. Random thoughts are meaningless, unless linked to other thoughts on some ordering criteria apart from the thoughts themselves. That ordering criteria is the orientation to truth.

To say it differently, the linkage between thoughts can be variously described as "caused," or "logical," or "making sense," but these all mean the same thing. One thought leads to another in a sequence that yields conclusions that "logically" follow from the premises. This is true not only for high-brow philosophical thoughts, but also for the sequences of thoughts that form the mental activity of our everyday lives. The reason thought A leads to thought B and not Z is that the orientation to truth links A to B. The A to B connection is made because the thoughts from A to B are in the causal chain leading to truth.

Of course we've all had those "what was I thinking" kind of moments, when we realize that thought A somehow got us to P or Q instead of B. The process was interrupted somehow, perhaps by fatigue, distraction, misunderstanding, faulty memory, or emotion. But generally, there is a connection between thoughts that makes sense to us, and that making of sense is rationality. We would say a thought is "irrational" if it isn't connected by logic to other thoughts, or the connection is untethered from the orientation to truth.

The materialist view of rationality is that it is the product of mere physical events of biochemistry. That is, the bridge from thought to thought is a material process only. Brain tissue and electricity alone link thoughts. The problem with this view is that it means a neuronal event (a physical electrical charge on the biological tissue of neurons) can occur as a result of physical necessity, but not logical necessity. Thought B would happen because thought A initiates a neuronal event leading to thought B. That isn't logic, that's physical causation.

Rationality requires a pre-existing logical syntax, a non-physical structure to link informational content which interacts with (and perhaps trains) physical neurons. When we say B follows "logically" from A, we invoke logic—the "logos," the word: information. The movement from thought A to B is governed by the content of information, not physical causation. Reasoning therefore cannot be the product of mere physical events of biochemistry. It is not enough to say, as materialists must, that physical interactions accumulate to the point that they can give rise to concepts. What is missing from such a formulation is that there had to be some conceptual framework in place before the first physical interaction could be given meaning. A conceptual structure has to be in the mind before even the first physical interaction. It is the conceptualization in the mind that enables successive logical inferences, not merely sensory inputs building upon experience of prior sensory inputs. Abstract thinking precedes experience, it is not solely the result of experience.

We can understand this by way of analogy to computers. A computer is not aware of the information it contains, of course, but in addition, in and of itself, a computer does not contain any semantic information at all. To say it differently, all the one's and zero's stored in silicon chips are not communication in themselves. They are merely physical markers, symbols, just like these letters in ink on this paper. The informational semantic content is not in the medium for the symbols, but in the intentional consciousness of the one who places the symbols, and the one who receives them.

The point is that there is no higher function within the computer to process the symbols, so that the computer becomes conscious of their content. We refer to a computer's "memory," but the word is misleading. A computer's "memory" is only the storage bank of symbols. No remembering takes place. The brain would work like a sophisticated computer, according to materialism. But no matter how sophisticated the seemingly brain-like computer, it would not think rationally, because of the absence of semantic content; of logical syntax; of conceptual framework, for ascribing meaning to the succession of physical markers. There is something more, to the brain.

Materialism holds that the mind is the same as the brain; that all of our mental activity is the product of physical processes in the brain. An idea by itself is obviously not material, however. It isn't made of organic compounds or electricity in a specific physical place. But materialism would nonetheless hold it is merely an emergent phenomenon of a particular combination of chemicals and tissue and electricity in the old noggin.

So if a thought isn't a combination of physical things, in what way is it connected to physical things? How is an immaterial thought connected to material?

We don't know. Clearly there is a physical component to our thinking, in the brain, but the features of thought and of consciousness and of mind seem so essentially different from physical features that it is difficult to see

CHAPTER 11: TRUTH AND RATIONALITY

how they connect. This is referred to in philosophy as the "mind-body problem;" the problem of sorting out how mental and physical properties interact. What is a thought, anyway? Is it physical? Does it reside somewhere? Is it connected to some place in our physical brain, and if so, how? Thoughts are the province of mind, and the mind is connected to the body (the brain) but how, exactly, is unknown.

Materialism supposes there are no mental (and no spiritual or soul-inhabited) states distinct from physical things. In some way as yet unexplained, it holds that a person's succession of thoughts proceed physically. Though the thought itself may be immaterial, it is nonetheless a property of the material brain.

This is difficult enough to imagine in a static situation, like a cartoon man with a thought balloon above his head. But it strains credulity that thought is only physical when we consider the dynamism of the thought process. Not just that there can be thought A followed rapidly by thought B, and so on; but that the *selection* of B to follow A is somehow also a physical process. It's one thing to imagine a thought tied to the brain, followed by another thought tied to the brain. It's quite another thing to imagine physical material *choosing* or *requiring* the second to follow the first.

Physical states of the brain cannot cause logic. Even if they support the thought, they do not support one thought leading logically, rationally, to another thought. A materialist might argue otherwise on the basis of determinism. Determinism, remember, is the idea that the physical state of anything at a particular moment is determined by all the physical states that preceded it. So the initial forces and material of the Big Bang determined everything that would happen thereafter, including the thought you're entertaining at this moment. Determinism is a necessary corollary of the materialist proposition, and it teaches that what will happen next is determined by the state of the universe now. Every event is caused by the combination of all the physical events that ever preceded it. Applying this to thought, one could say thought B emerges from a physical state which was inevitably and necessarily caused by the physical state from which thought A emerged. Only in this strictly deterministic sense might a materialist argue that there is a connection from thought to thought.

The problem with this theory is that it dispenses with the logical connection between thoughts. If the state of matter in the universe (including, most pertinently, the material of my brain) dictates what my next thought will be, then that is not a rational thought, but an irrational one. Thought

B might have the appearance of a logical connection to A, but it simply doesn't. Thought A physically, rather than rationally, caused B. If the A to B connection was not rational, it was irrational.

The rational linkage from thought to thought poses a particular difficulty for the materialist position. If we can imagine a thought as emerging somehow from one brain-state, and then the next thought as emerging somehow from an immediately subsequent brain-state, how could the physical change yield a transition from thought to thought that is rational? We would have to suppose that the rational connection between the thoughts results from the nature of the relationship of the underlying physical states. This throws us back onto truth orientation as some sort of substrate within which all physical brain activity occurs; a sort of cloud of rationality distinct from brain but within which tissue and electricity operates. This would have to be a kind of substrate of truth spoken into the world by universal Mind, imparting rationality to lesser human minds in the uncountable rational inferences made in every waking moment. This belies a materialist explanation for rationality.

If we examine materialism on its own merits, it appears to be self-defeating. In the course of thinking through materialism as an explanation of reality, one is engaged in rational thought. But that rational thought does not employ physical processes as required by materialism. Instead it involves rational, immaterial processes. There is not some combination of chemicals or electricity in the brain that causes me to write this sentence in a way that makes it logically follow the preceding sentence. Nor is there a combination of chemicals or electricity in your brain to cause you to ascribe logic or illogic to what I write. Not only that, but if our actions are determined by physics alone, there is no assurance of arriving at truth. The determinant for the content of a thought is not truth, but the complex combination of physical vectors comprising the state of material at the moment the thought is formed.

The existence of rational inferences experienced subjectively would appear to be among the most basic of our beliefs about reality. To deny them runs counter to our very sense of subjective directedness—the "aboutness" of our consciousness; its intentionality. How can we exist as mere meat machines or organic calculators, when we have this deep intuition that inside our minds we make rational inferences from observation to idea, or idea to idea? We employ rational inferences even to discern the truth or falsity of the proposition that rational inferences explain reality.

Chapter 12: **Consciousness**

Mind over matter

THERE IS A MYSTERY at the base of all of our ruminations about consciousness. That sense of mystery resists reduction to material causes. Material reality is ultimately dependent upon mind, because any encounter we have with natural reality occurs through the medium of our consciousness, a product of our mind, which relates to the mind of God which preceded and brought into being the material reality we encounter.

Materialism assumes the reverse: that manifestations of mind, being in this instance only the human mind, originated in material, such as in this speculation: A flash of electricity in a primordial pond caused amino acids to form which coalesced into lipid membranes which evolved to cells which evolved to Albert Einstein, Mother Teresa, the 9/11 terrorists, and you.

But if material produced mind, rather than the other way around, then our consciousness would be a passive receptor of external stimuli. We would be bombarded with perception of meaningless events, one after another, which would make no larger sense at all. These formulations of "mind over matter" and "matter over mind" are important to grasp because they are shorthand for fundamentally different ways of seeing reality. The first is the "top-down" theist view of reality. The second is the materialist "bottom-up" view of reality.

If the "mind over matter" or "top-down" point of view is correct, then Mind precedes matter and is predominant over matter and is more immediate than matter. Physical creation is a product of infinite and eternal Mind; the mind of God. Man exists primarily as mind within the physical world, though that mind is at least in this life connected to the physical body. Just how is yet but poorly understood—it is the "mind/body problem" of philosophy. Being created by God, man has an intuition of God's presence and the particular features of his own conscious mind echo those of God's. They may be connected in some way poorly understood, in this life in the body. Though physical features of the cosmos may evolve or change, and though there are certainly mechanistic or natural processes in play, physical things are ultimately subordinate to a universal Mind, which supervenes upon nature.

The "matter over mind" or "bottom-up" point of view is atheistic; or, to avoid saying what it isn't instead of what it is: materialistic or naturalistic. If the materialist view is correct, the origin of physical things and the physical laws acting upon them are inexplicable and the origin of first life is at best a deep mystery, but the existence of the current state of physical things is nonetheless deemed explainable entirely as the outworking of physical processes acting on physical things. Mind, on this view, is an emergent property of the material brain, in the same way that a beautiful landscape is said to emerge from a particular combination of pigments applied to canvas.

Remember the primary competitor to theism in this age is materialism. Materialism imagines an essentially mechanistic universe. From the current physical state of the universe, we could extrapolate to future states of the universe, down to the smallest detail, if we have sufficient information about the current physical state. Another way of saying this is that if there was one pin-point of beginning, at the Big Bang, then all subsequent physical states in the universe were determined at that point, including the physical states which constitute your being at this moment. On this view, material forces are inherently mindless and intrinsically devoid of purpose, as are all the material states that result, including human beings.

But our consciousness is purpose-driven in every conscious moment of our lives. Consciousness poses such a big problem for the naturalism worldview because it has features which that mechanistic vision cannot account for. Materialism precludes meaning, purpose, and directedness to human conduct. But consciousness is the opposite: directed, purposive, and rational. For many thinkers, human consciousness is conclusive on the question whether there is a reality beyond that which is merely physical. So many features of consciousness appear inexplicable from a purely physical standpoint.

Subjectivity

Physical states are not private, but are open to inspection, so to speak. Anyone can look in on them and make such sense of them as they can.

CHAPTER 12: CONSCIOUSNESS

Imagine freezing time, and then opening up the cranium to examine the status of neurons, synapses, and electrical stimuli in that frozen moment. You would see the physical state of the brain. Mental states, however, are private. No amount of looking into the brain will reveal the private subjective sensory and mental impressions in the consciousness of the poor individual in this thought experiment.

This private, subjective experience includes the irreducibly subjective feeling of "what it is like" to experience something. Pain, for example, might be caused by some exterior, objective instrumentality, but the subjective experience of that pain is not an objective item open to general scrutiny. You may see me hit my thumb with a hammer, but you don't experience the pain that results.

This subjective experience is essential for the encounter of and mental registering of any physical phenomenon. Internally, and privately, we mentally differentiate among the physical phenomena we encounter. We internally sort through the myriad sense impressions we are constantly bombarded with. In fact, all of the physical phenomena we encounter are processed through, or filtered by, our subjective conscious processes. No appreciation of physical reality can occur other than through the medium of our consciousness. It lies between our private mental states and the objective physical states of the world. Through it we perceive reality, and that perception is active on our part. In our mental states we project outward onto that reality. It is made comprehensible not only by its own intrinsic order, but by the rational process we bring to bear in perceiving it. The world makes sense through our interaction with it over the medium of our consciousness.

In the philosophy of consciousness there is the concept of "intentionality." It does not mean volition or exercise of the will, but rather the outward-directedness of one's consciousness. It is sometimes referred to as the "aboutness" of consciousness. Our consciousness is not merely a passive mental reception of sensory data fed into the rational mechanisms of the brain. Rather, the mind has the power to direct itself toward something. The mind orients itself toward a specific object, purpose, or end. Sensory impressions are not raw data, but rather a product themselves of the mind's directedness toward external objective phenomena. There is an interactivity between the sense impression and the mind's directedness in perceiving it. The mind actively imposes on the perception an idea of what that sensory perception is about.

Materialists hold that physical reality just is; that it is devoid of purpose or meaning in and of itself. It is therefore not directed toward any ends at all, therefore no element of intent is in play. If naturalism were true, then all physical events that intrude onto our awareness would be perceived as distinct, unconnected, and random. But they aren't. Our consciousness orders those events in such a way that we derive meaning from them.

Prior content

Physical reality external to the self is not discerned merely as a fact of physical presence. One's consciousness brings abstract concepts concerning that physical reality to bear, in perceiving it. Consider a buzzing bee, hovering around a flower. In one's consciousness, it is perceived as a discrete object; as an object of a particular type; as an object taxonomically distinct from other objects; and so on. All of these are categorical distinctions brought to bear upon the physical object so as to render it understandable. These categories are provided by abstract conceptualization in the consciousness. We don't merely obtain a sensory impression of the bee. Some notion of form must pre-exist the sensory perception.

A materialist might argue that the forms which enable these categories of thought derive from experience reduced to physical form; the accumulation of sensory impressions and learning from them over time, giving rise to the forms of thought. The trouble with that argument, however, is that before those sense impressions begin to accumulate, there has to be some prior existing conscious framework for those accumulating sense impressions. The materialist view of synthesizing accumulations of experiential data is not possible without some prior conceptual framework pre-existing the accumulation of data.

Consciousness must be in part distinct from the physical component of mental events for us to have any continuous experience of anything at all. Certain categories of the mind are not connected to particular things, but are instead abstractly applicable to all things. The mind can abstractly conceive of the perfect isosceles triangle, but no perfect isosceles triangle exists in physical reality. And yet, when perceiving a physical triangle, we readily categorize it with the form already abstractly held by us in our consciousness. Similarly, the concept of causation is a pre-existing category of mind. We may perceive smoke rising from a fire, and conclude that the fire causes the smoke. We might be familiar with heat and combustibility, but we could still make no sense of smoke rising from a fire without the prior concept of causation. We observe sequence, but the conscious mind provides *con*sequence. Causation is not merely a learned feature of the physical world. We observe A followed by B followed by C, but the causal link among them is a prior abstraction not derived from mere observation. Mathematical concepts, and abstract concepts such as beauty and justice, or intelligible ideas like infinity, or the grasping of logical truths, or fantasy and fancy and speculative thought; or letting one concept lead to another under its own momentum—all of these are beyond explanation from a purely materialist explanation of reality.

The thought category of causation may be described as a part of the "logos," or informational content that necessarily precedes our reception of sensory inputs in the brain, so that we perceive things as making sense. Rather than being constantly bombarded by random impressions of colors, sounds, feel, smell, and taste, we are able to mentally construct them into a unified whole; to make sense of them. If I walk through an unfamiliar forest, my surroundings do not present as mere random swatches of colorful light, because I bring to the experience not only memory of similar experiences, but also these elements of consciousness: intentionality, rationality, and abstracted concepts like causation. And then my present sense impressions are connected by rational thought, creating a comprehensible order in my surroundings. Materialism cannot explain these features of consciousness.

Other awareness

There is a social element to our consciousness, too. You've probably known someone who shows signs of being socially awkward because he's "self-conscious." Perhaps you've experienced it yourself. A person becomes "self-conscious" not merely because he has the fundamental features of individual consciousness, but rather because of a peculiar collective feature of consciousness, which makes us aware, sometimes too intensely, that we are perceived by others with the same kind of intentionality of consciousness that we ourselves possess.

"Self-awareness" is a phrase sometimes used as a kind of short-hand for consciousness, but it's too limited. One is "self-aware" in that, while he is thinking about what he wants on his hamburger, he is also aware of himself thinking about what he wants on his hamburger. It is a third-person point of view that we can adopt at will. It enables us to conceptualize God, and indeed many theorize that it is the point of departure between the consciousness of humans and animals. We are self-aware creatures, meaning that we are aware of being aware. But a person is not merely self-aware, he is also other-aware. We are not merely aware of another person's presence, but aware of another person's also having self-awareness. A kind of double-feedback can then occur, in which I am aware of your awareness of my awareness. This seems to be an essential element of human consciousness, in fact—so much so that in utter isolation we wither in ways only beginning to be understood. Prolonged segregation in prison, for example, has only recently come to be seen as little short of torture. We can say this is evidence that we're social animals, and that's certainly true, but how is that manifested in us individually? It would seem to be manifested in this double-awareness that is so much a feature of human consciousness.

To ascend to yet another level of abstraction, if we have third-person self-awareness—such as I have in my awareness of your awareness of me—why wouldn't that third-person self-awareness extend to entities other than the people around us? That is, if we can imagine an awareness outside ourselves, we can further imagine that awareness to be held by another Being; one who, by virtue of this awareness, is super-sentient rather than merely another like me. That super-sentient Being might have mutual awareness of me, as I do in company with other people. And that super-sentient Being might have vastly greater awareness, as by knowing me better than I know myself. And that knowing might be a necessary feature of an all-knowing and all-caring and all-powerful being. That is, God: omniscient, omnibenevolent, omnipotent.

Third-person awareness

But is this an exercise of imagination only? It seems doubtful, because the all-seeing eye perspective is so universal in human experience, and because it seems a necessary extrapolation of the features of consciousness we have. There has to be such a Being to do the interacting with us that these elements of our consciousness require.

Look at a painting or photograph which depicts a scene with which you are familiar. Maybe a vacation photo. Now try to exclude the actual scene from your imagination, and focus on the photo by itself. What is it? It is a two-dimensional arrangement of colors. It represents visually something

CHAPTER 12: CONSCIOUSNESS

else, a physical reality that exists in four dimensions: length, width, depth, and time. But it is not itself that four-dimensional reality.

Now imagine that your world consisted only of the two-dimensional visual. Suppose you existed in *Flatland*, as imagined by Edwin Abbott in his book with that title. Try to limit your appreciation of reality to being only what the photograph represents, and other photographs like it. All around you is a two-dimensional reality: length and width, spatially; static and frozen temporally. If that had always been the totality of what you perceived, wouldn't it be hard to imagine the third dimension of space, depth? And wouldn't it be harder still to imagine those three spatial dimensions changing dynamically, as they're swept along by time?

Look at the photo and imagine that being the entirety of your perception. And then, imagine that photo opening out into the third dimension, like a picture of a person transforming itself into a sculpture. And then imagine the scene changing with time, as with the sculpture bending and moving. And then imagine the moving sculpture having life and other-awareness like yours, and yourself able to move about and adjust your perspective, so that more and more of the four-dimensional physical world comes alive to you. You're back in the physical reality we perceive every day.

Could there be still more? What if there is yet another dimension, but our ability to perceive it is limited, in the same way yours was when you imagined you lived in the two-dimensional reality of that photograph. What if, moreover, that additional dimension is created and occupied by a Being (a first and fully actualized Being) which has life and sentient other-awareness? Suppose that Being's awareness was different in kind than the awareness of another person, such that he is not only aware of our awareness, as other people are, but also shared our private, interior world with us, breaching the wall between private subjective mental states, and objective physical states.

Perhaps expressed this way the idea of heaven, and of God inhabiting it, is more accessible to us. We "imagine" such a thing because we have the capacity to place in our minds the "image" of an unseen reality, and by reason we can arrive at an understanding as to how that unseen reality is a reasonable extrapolation from the physical reality we accept as given; even a necessary extrapolation.

"Self-awareness," is too simple a term to serve as a synonym for consciousness. Self-awareness refers to the fact that we think, but while we're thinking, we're thinking about the fact that we're thinking. But actually our self-awareness is much more complicated even than that. We can think of self-awareness on four levels. The first level is simply one's awareness of physical things around him. There are objects in our environment; we perceive them and consider them subjectively. The philosopher Roger Scruton (and others) use the language of "subject" and "object" which is helpful. When you perceive things, you do so subjectively. You are the subject, and the things you perceive are objects.

The second level begins to explain the social nature of human beings. We have subject to subject awareness, when we understand that other people have the same kind of self-awareness we do. My self-awareness includes an awareness that you have self-awareness.

The third level involves subject-to-subject interaction: intersubjectivity. Your self-awareness includes an awareness that I have awareness of your self-awareness. Your self-awareness loops back on itself, so to speak. You are aware of my presence, and you're aware that I have self-awareness like you, but in addition, you are aware specifically of my awareness of your awareness. Without trying, we see ourselves through the eyes of others. One implication of this third-level self-awareness is that there is an instant social dynamic; a new shared reality that is distinct from what was in the individual subjective consciousness. All parties to the social interaction are conscious of a shared culture, more or less developed, because of the mutual self-awareness. Society-wide, this explains the shared cultural memory to which we are heir. It also explains *zeitgeist*—the spirit of the age—which is current shared cultural awareness. We live in the moment but also have memory. Socially, we have shared mutual awareness in the moment, but also shared mutual awareness of our collective past. It is this shared mutual awareness that at times builds into a societal tension requiring release in scapegoating individuals or minority groups. This is among the frailties of organized mankind that Jesus exposed by being scapegoated himself, yet rising literally above it all. Rene Girard, in his *I Saw Satan Fall Like Lightning* (1999) insightfully explains this phenomenon.

The fourth level gets at how one understands religion. Even while participating in the shared culture of interacting with other people, there is still a part of one's self-awareness that is private. Some thoughts remain yours alone. I may make inferences about what you are thinking based on what you say and do, but your innermost thoughts remain private. The moral compass, the conscience, applies to those private thoughts and actions just as it does to those expressed or visible to other people. We respond to pangs of conscience even though the relevant thoughts and actions are private because we acquire a perspective that goes even beyond person-to-person third-level self-awareness. We adopt the perspective of a sentient entity so powerful that even private thoughts and actions are open to it; our own and everyone else's, because we are self-aware that everyone else, too, has a conscience. The question is whether the explanation ends there, or whether this social feature of consciousness exists because a creator God is the Author of it.

We feel it instinctively that we are known. We endlessly store up guilt if we think it stays locked up privately forever. Something more than simply being discovered in our fault is going on. Confession, repentance, apology are soul-healing activities for a reason. We have an instinct against burying our wrongs. A sense that, left buried, they will fester and make us ill. This derives from the instinct that we are known; even within that interiority not open to other people. We are known by God, and we are aware of His knowing, on a deep level.

Love

I suggest a connection between the phenomena of consciousness discussed here, and another phenomenon we obsess over but little understand: love. The subject-to-subject connection—intersubjectivity—is certainly real, and it's also something we yearn for. It's necessary, even, to our well-being as human beings. We find isolation to be debilitating, as innumerable studies show, and as we've all experienced on some level. Loneliness is painful, and love is the cure.

A feature of this intersubjectivity we so desire is that we are conscious of being *known*. In the presence of another person, we know that other person knows us. It is an element of that third-level consciousness mentioned above. I am aware of your awareness of my awareness. We *know* each other. Perhaps the strength of that knowing is weak, as when we're among slight acquaintances, but it may be stronger, as when we're in the company of a close friend or spouse or sibling.

Imagine being a celebrity. Perhaps a famous actor who—whatever else you might say about him or her—is *known*. Could this be the draw that so many have to achieving fame? Or imagine young lovers, each infatuated with the other. It's not just worship from afar, like the admiration one might have for that famous actor. Instead, an essential element of that swooning head-over-heels feeling we have in the throes of new romantic love is a deep sense of being *known*. The relationship infatuates because of the newness of being *known* more deeply than in other kinds of relationships; more deeply especially because of the mutual expectation of exclusivity which drives the depths of that knowing.

We described consciousness itself as being defined in part by the phenomenon of intersubjecivity. Our self-awareness incorporates our perception of what others think of us as self-aware beings. The social component of our being is ineluctable because it is not just sort of the way people are. It is a feature of our very consciousness as human beings. The awareness play-back arises because of our deep desire to be known, so we can say that being known, also, is integral to our very consciousness. The yearning to be known can be analogized to the gravitational pull between bodies, that we know of through physics. We can label that gravitational pull "love." We don't love everyone, obviously, nor is our love of the same kind or intensity among those we do love. The kind of love we feel and its intensity depends on the nature of the relationship and proximity and duration. We might be better off with many more words to describe those feelings for others, than just "love," but perhaps having the one word is useful in this context, because we can correctly say that love, in the abstract, is what binds us to other people. That binding effect in the consciousness of every person arises from our individual desire to be *known*. Opening oneself to another like me, who knows me, is love, or an essential element of love, at least.

This desire to open oneself to be known is not absolute, of course. In fact there is a tension, wherein we desire to hold back some of ourselves in the ultimate interiority of our consciousness, where no other person can peer in. That is the repository for our secrets, the ugly little things we want no one to see, kept even from our dearest beloved, the one to whom we are most open to being known and therefore the one we most love.

If we can imagine a first, second, and third level of consciousness, establishing the full playback intersubjectivity of human mutual awareness, and extrapolate from there to a fourth level, involving One who breaches even that secret wall of interiority, the corresponding love toward that omniscient One would be that much more than the love toward another person. And it would be a response to the love directed first from that One, to whom we are so thoroughly known.

If you have a (U.S.) dollar bill, take it out and look at the back side of it. See the pyramid with the eye above it? It is the all-seeing eye, a

CHAPTER 12: CONSCIOUSNESS

non-sectarian representation of God. It symbolizes his omniscience. He sees even into that reserved space of interiority. If God is as understood by the Jews and then Christians, he knows us entirely. We respond either with the love that accompanies yielding to that knowing, or with resistance, perhaps even resentfulness, that we are known so thoroughly. Our resistance may take the form of denying the very existence of the Knower, as if pretending he is not there prevents his penetration of our illusory god-like sovereignty. We may so desire the impregnability of our self-made castle that we imagine out of existence the Besieger.

If this thesis is correct—that our consciousness incorporates the desire to be known and thereby the ability to receive and give love—then with respect to God there would seem to be no middle ground. He knows us even interiorly, and his love for us corresponds to that knowing, in that its depth and intensity is beyond our considerable imagining. His love for us is not lukewarm. Ours for him may be, however, because of the tension between our wanting to reserve unto ourselves an ineradicable kernel of self, even as against our creator, and our desire to give in entirely to love; to be ravished by it. We hold onto self because we would be gods ourselves.

By giving in to God's full knowing, however, we embrace also the fullness of his love and thereby a greater capacity in ourselves to love others. What we are ever learning is that by giving ourselves over to his love, to the last, we don't actually give up that last reserved grain of self after all. Instead, and paradoxically, we gain a grander self than we are presently able to imagine. We behave like the proverbial monkey that reaches into a jar and grabs a treat, but with fist clenched can't remove its hand through the narrow neck of the jar. It has the treat but can't enjoy it, and is captured because of the tight-fisted hanging on to self. We none of us are completely freed from this grasping capture while in life. We live inside that moment of indecision between grasping and releasing. One must lose his life to gain life, the Bible tells us. Perhaps we completely perceive this only in heaven. But in our present, partial understanding, we can at least intellectually purpose to yield to his love, and find we are better able to love others.

In this way we draw closer to, and become more like, the Lover of our souls. God is self-actualized and fully-actualized Being. By modeling ourselves on him we become more fully actualized ourselves. Or as the Bible has it, we live life "abundantly." Love is the solvent for that actualization, and love comes from being known, the yearning for which is an ineluctable element of human consciousness. By being known by God and returning that love through ever-increasing searching out of the character of God, we advance to the goal that in him we "live and move and have our being," as we read in Acts 17:28. The binding element of this unity is love, just as lesser loves are the binding element of unity between or among people.

We can infer that heroes of faith like Abraham were strong in their belief not only because of the profound evidence to which even we have access, but also because they felt the presence of God's knowing, to which they responded in love. Perhaps Abraham had first-hand experience of that mutual knowing but now, following the Christ's Ascension, we're left without, so that we develop that intersubjectivity with others, with the Helper, the Holy Spirit. And then, recognize in that intersubjectivity the love that comes from being known and then apply that understanding to intersubjectivity with God. This would partially explain the emphasis on prayer, in the Bible.

This might help explain the difficulty Christians have about what "belief" in God means. It means something more than intellectual assent. The various references to "believing" in Jesus as God imply taking some sort of risk. But what does that mean, for a well-fed Westerner who seems to want for nothing because he doesn't perceive his spiritual starvation? Are we to purposely seek out misery, in this life, like modern Stylites? Are we to line up for the religious persecutions that emerge from time to time? I suggest the "risk" factor involved in belief means a yielding to the fact of being known by God in the entire interior portion of our consciousness. It is the risk of yielding the self to the unknown, trusting that that unknown is as represented to us in God's revelation. The problem is that what we really want is invisible to us, and becomes visible only when we give up our most cherished possession: the petulant little tyrant who lives in the heart and wants things his way.

Chapter 13: **Knowledge, Belief, Faith**

How does anyone know anything? What propositions do we accept as true, and why? How do we formulate beliefs about things not directly knowable? To begin to answer these questions, we should first get our terms straight. (This is pretty much always the right starting point). There is potential for confusion among seemingly simple words like "knowledge," "belief," and "faith."

We say we *know* things because we observe them. We observe them because they are "sensible" to us; that is, presented to our senses of sight, sound, and so on. We see or hear or otherwise physically observe something, and on that basis are likely to say we "know" the thing observed to be true.

But do we? Suppose we only think we're observing and experiencing things, but it's all in our head? Maybe the neuronal events associated with observations and experiences are occurring, but not the experiences themselves. Maybe we are experiencing things only internally; like a head in a jar attached only to neuronal stimulants. This might sound like silly philosopher-twaddle, but it actually serves to introduce the subject of epistemology: theories for how one can know anything. We generally trust the evidence of our senses, but should we? They register in our mind, but what is the mind? A medium for transition from physical sensation to thought? Or something more?

Just as we tend to think we "know" things by direct observation, we also extend that knowing to conclusions we confidently reach through the exercise of our reason. It's one thing to trust a conclusion reached by direct observation through the senses; something else to trust a conclusion arrived at by the exercise of reason. The more we build inference upon inference, the more opportunities to be mistaken. I may "know" it is raining because I see water falling from the sky, for example. But suppose I'm inside where I can't see out. I might still infer rain because the air is cooler and more damp, and the light less strong. In that instance the observation is not direct. To reach the same conclusion (that it is raining) I must apply reason to my current senses and my memory of similar sensations in the past.

We can imagine evidence still more attenuated from the sense observations. I might conclude it is raining because you tell me it is. In that instance, I'm not trusting my sense observations at all, except in the limited sense that I hear the sound of your voice and mentally interpret the sounds into words that carry meaning. Hearing is a sense, but it's not rain I hear, it's your report of rain. It's sound I mentally reduce to information. To conclude for myself that it's raining, I'd have to trust that you have valid reasons for your conclusion and are truthful. Perhaps you saw water fall from the sky, but perhaps you only heard this information from some unreliable source. You might even be purposely misleading me.

Things we "know" can be quite removed from direct observation, and more or less dependent on reasoned inferences rather than direct observation. In addition, without pausing to consider how, we easily shift gears in the mental process to adjust for the level of importance of the subject matters on which we reach conclusions.

The foregoing is about "knowing" something. Let's now shift to "belief." It seems inescapable that there is a sliding scale for how confidently we say we know something to be true or false. If I believe it's raining because I observed it, I'd say I "know" it's raining, but I could as easily say I "believe" it's raining. To be sure, my belief would be quite strong in that instance, because experience tells me there's a near-100-percent correlation between the evidence of water falling from the sky, and the fact of rain. But if I'm away from a window and I'm considering lesser evidence—coolness and dampness of air, dimmer reflected sunlight, perhaps a background noise that could be but may not be rain—my degree of conviction for the belief is going to be something less than 100 percent.

So let's consider this in the context of religion, specifically theism, and even more specifically, orthodox Christianity. "Faith," as we read in Hebrews 11:1, is "the assurance of things hoped for, the conviction of things not seen." This is a good statement of the sliding scale of confidence one might have in what he thinks he knows. "Assurance" and "conviction" denote a high level of confidence. The context for this verse is the truth of our hoped-for resurrection in Christ, and necessary to that, the truth of the Gospel story which includes a reality beyond nature; that is, "things not seen." Faith, then, is not a binary on/off switch, but rather a degree

CHAPTER 13: KNOWLEDGE, BELIEF, FAITH

of confidence in one's conclusions from the evidence. Like light, it can be bright or dim or any level of intensity in-between.

Christianity holds that genuine faith requires a degree of conviction stronger than mere intellectual assent. This is apparent from the many scriptural references to "belief" as entailing action in reliance on the truth of the "things hoped for." The many Bible references to "belief" contemplate belief inducing changed conduct, consistent with a high degree of conviction that the Gospel story is true.

The subject matter of that belief may not seem immediate, however. Our survival from one moment to the next does not appear to depend on whether we subscribe to theism or atheism. The subject matter of both is eternity and our place in it. A person who disavows God altogether may live this present life in a way that is not appreciably different than does a Christian. The result is that though we are presented with mutually exclusive sets of metaphysical propositions (theism and materialism) on the most important question there is, it may seem that we can indefinitely put off resolving it.

How important it might be that we come to a correct conclusion depends on subject matter. Suppose the subject is the weather. It might not matter much whether it's raining or not at the moment. It may be inconsequential whether one has a strong or weak belief in the state of the weather, or whether one forms a belief about it at all. But if the question is whether there is a God, the implications are large. The consequences of getting it wrong are significant, though they may not seem immediate.

One more thing should be said, in this context, about what belief is. Or is *not*, more precisely. Belief describes the range of confidence, from weak to strong, that one may have in the truth of a proposition. It is not, however, a substitute for the proposition itself. If I believe it is raining, that doesn't mean it actually is raining; nor that it isn't. It could be raining right now whether I believe it is or not. This may seem obvious, but it's an important distinction to make because sometimes this confusion does exist, especially when it comes to religion. So let's restate this point using Christianity. If I believe the Gospel story, that doesn't make it true. And if I disbelieve the Gospel story, that doesn't make it false. It is true or false independently of what I think of it. The truth or falsity of the Gospel does not depend on whether I accept it or reject it.

Moreover, it is true or false if I form no belief at all. The evidence cannot lead to a conclusion that the Gospel is *neither* true nor false. It cannot be both; it cannot be neither. So if I ignore the Gospel or remain irresolute about its truth or falsity, I form no belief at all about true facts, whatever they are. There are only these four possibilities: (a) I believe the Gospel and it is true; (b) I believe the Gospel and it is false; (c) I don't believe the Gospel and it is true; and (d) I don't believe the Gospel and it is false.

	The Gospel is true	The Gospel is false
I believe the Gospel	(a)	(b)
I disbelieve the Gospel	(c)	(d)

Only these four possibilities exist. The four finite possibilities each have profound significance. Possibility (a) is a top-down view of God, and imbues a sense of meaning and purpose. Possibilities (b) and (d) would mean there is no ultimate meaning, and the existentialist and hedonistic philosophers are right, there is no point to living beyond maximizing pleasure and minimizing pain. Possibility (c) means eternal separation from the only Source of meaning. It makes sense, if one is irresolute, to consider the consequences of irresolution. It can be the result of confusion between the concepts of belief and truth.

Coherentism

Another instance of confusion between belief and truth is in the philosophical approach to belief known as "coherentism." It is a model for how one comes to hold his particular set of beliefs. The idea is that in an effort to construct a comprehensive picture of how things work, we adopt belief systems based on beliefs we already hold, so that the resulting belief systems cohere more or less consistently.

One could readily come up with a defense of coherentism by considering one's own beliefs and how one evaluates ideas in the culture on the basis of those existing beliefs. Suppose, for example, you have a strong belief that work and economic independence are necessary components of human dignity. You would likely disapprove legal or cultural movements tending toward socialism. If you believe socialism is a natural state for societies because people are social creatures, you would be more likely to approve expansion of government programs in an otherwise capitalist, free-trade society. The

CHAPTER 13: KNOWLEDGE, BELIEF, FAITH

idea is that there are common threads running through our belief system, which cause different combinations of beliefs to cohere intelligibly and consistently. Expressed in this way, coherentism seems like a common-sense and innocuous description of how we come to believe things. But if we pursue the logic behind coherentism, we find that it incorporates some startling assumptions about the nature of reality.

The best way to understand the significance of coherentism is to contrast it with "foundationalism." Foundationalism explains beliefs as being justified on the basis of how they correspond to some objective, absolute truth. The same basic idea is expressed in philosophy as a "correspondence theory" of truth. The idea is that one's beliefs are formed on the basis of how they correspond to true things about the world. Beliefs build upon one another on the criterion of their fidelity to more foundational beliefs that underlie them, and which correspond to true facts in the world external to one's thought processes. Foundationalism supposes there are such objective and absolute foundational truths, so our project is to go out and discover them and form our beliefs accordingly. Science is an example. It is a process for discovering truths about the material world, and it depends on certain more foundational truths, such as there being order in the universe, and our senses being reliable as we go about experimenting and testing hypotheses. If foundationalism remains an accurate model of how we form our beliefs, then it is correct to regard our beliefs as true or not true. Truth is the sole criterion for considering a belief justified.

If on the other hand coherentism is a correct model for how we come to hold our beliefs, then we must throw out notions of ultimate truth, including the whole scientific endeavor. We must abandon any notion that our beliefs correspond to anything true. Beliefs are acquired not because they are true, but because they seem to cohere with already-held beliefs. Rationality is a casualty. "Coherency" implies rational thought, and we might say rational thought connects an acquired belief to an existing belief. But the existing belief needn't be rational. An entire edifice of coherent beliefs may rest upon a few core beliefs that are simply wrong and irrational.

Moreover, each person's constellation of beliefs would be self-contained. Truth itself would seem to be the first casualty because the criterion for holding a belief is one's other beliefs, not a hard-wired orientation toward truth. Beliefs and not truths would be authoritative, hence confusion between belief and fact. If coherentism provides an accurate picture of how we come to believe things, then our perception of an orientation to truth is illusory.

One's beliefs are an accident of biological make-up combined with individual experience; not a product of reasoning to objective truth.

Because coherentism holds that beliefs are based not on truth, but on other beliefs, religious belief can be disregarded because belief in a deity merely coheres with other beliefs, like the belief that people are bad and therefore in need of a savior, and that consciousness of death induces in us an ameliorative belief in an afterlife. Coherentism thus serves as a tool for attempting to dismantle religious belief.

One of the ironies of coherentism is that it argues as true that truth is irrelevant. If existing belief, rather than truth, is the criterion for adopting a new belief, then on what basis is coherentism adopted? Not truth, perforce, but belief. An individual can be in agreement with another only insofar as their constellations of belief overlap. So if one's picture of how we come to "know" things is coherentism, that means there is no common thread through society; we are each an island unto ourselves. Each of us a separate constellation of beliefs. How could an idea come to prevail across society, if coherentism is a correct model for how we develop beliefs? Not by common deference to objective truth, but only through persuasion and coercion. If we consider beliefs to be only constellations of like beliefs, rather than corresponding to objective truth, then the beliefs that prevail across society will be only those that survive an ideological struggle for dominance.

Presumption

It's easy to be dismissive of someone's beliefs as being something they've acquired unthinkingly, or as a necessary piece of a systematic dogma, as with specific religious creeds. Sometimes people do acquire beliefs they subscribe to without a lot of understanding. But then, it seems inevitable that it be so. From our first moments of awareness, as infants, we observe and reason and thereby begin to acquire beliefs about the reality around us. The beliefs are not in every instance the subject of careful analysis and scrutiny as if we could somehow approach them with no pre-conceived ideas at all. Everyone believes something, including something about ultimate questions of metaphysics, like whether God is or not.

Let's re-introduce the notion of neutrality, therefore. Is it ever possible to evaluate a metaphysical proposition (for example that there is or is not a God) from a position of neutrality? One has to start somewhere. If we think critically about the evidence for God's existence, we do so from a belief or at

CHAPTER 13: KNOWLEDGE, BELIEF, FAITH

least a working assumption that there is no God. If we think critically about the evidence for materialism, we do so from a belief or at least a working assumption that God exists. To evaluate any proposition, we put that proposition in the dock, so to speak, so as to evaluate it. We evaluate the proposition by supposing its opposite to be true, in order to test it.

This may sound like a silly illustration, but suppose you hear on the news that the sun rose in the east this morning. Of course the sun rose in the east. It always does. Large physical forces are at work in causing a consistent eastern sunrise; they won't suddenly reverse on a particular day. The only surprise is that it made the news. We don't examine critically the eastern sunrise report, because we already hold the belief that it occurred just as reported. (We might examine critically *why* it was reported, but that's another matter.) Now suppose the opposite: it's reported that the sun rose this morning in the west. *That* proposition we would examine critically. Pretty much anyone's starting belief is going to be the opposite of the western sunrise proposition. The point is that any proposition that seriously comes to our attention for evaluation is going to be examined against its opposition. That's what critical thinking is, and "critical thinking" is a good thing. It's what we do as human beings. It is normal, rational, reasoning. If someone says the sun rose in the east, you evaluate it as one who believes the sun rises in the east. Likewise if someone says it rose in the west. You evaluate it as one who believes the sun rises in the east. We don't evaluate the eastern sunrise proposition critically. We do evaluate the western sunrise proposition critically. In both instances, we have a pre-existing belief on the subject matter. We are not neutral on the question of sunrise orientation.

Questions that present to our mind for evaluation do so because they stand in opposition to our expectation. If a person holds a belief that no supernatural reality animates the natural world, the God proposition will have to be proven to him. We would say that person imposes a burden of proof on the God proposition. If a person holds a belief that there is an unseen, non-physical realm inhabited by God that runs in and through the natural world, the burden of proof rests on the materialist proposition. There is no reason to say that either the atheism or the theism point of view carries a burden of proof in the abstract.

We have a tendency to criticize someone for not backing up his beliefs with what we consider to be sufficient proofs, all the while unable to defend our own, and perhaps not even being conscious of our own. It's easy to suppose, for example, that religious people have beliefs, but skeptics don't. But that's silly. Skeptics hold beliefs too, on the same subject matter. This isn't hard to prove. It's what it means to be a skeptic. One cannot be a skeptic in the abstract. Skepticism necessarily relates to a particular subject matter. If you say there's a God and I say there isn't, we're both voicing opinions on the same subject. There is no reason that one set of views and not the other should be considered presumptively valid. There is no reason, therefore, that one side should have the "burden of proof" as to his point of view.

People may be confused in this way because they're used to describing their belief as "agnostic" or "atheist," both words being descriptions of what they aren't, instead of what they are. They choose words indicating they consider themselves merely not-knowing, or non-theist, instead of acknowledging that they have a metaphysical perspective that is just as much a substantive belief as that of a theist. If a person thinks all of reality is physical or a property of that which is physical, then he has adopted an anti-metaphysical doctrinal stance. Such a person is a naturalist, or a materialist, or a physicalist; not merely a *non*-something. Abetting this illusion of neutrality even further is the borrowing of theistic concepts into an atheistic paradigm. Concepts of teleology, inspiration, transcendence, and the moral primacy of human life are routinely smuggled in where they don't belong: to justifications for a naturalistic worldview.

Another way of saying this is to merely observe that we don't really figure out what's true and then start living accordingly. We live according to assumptions about reality that we absorb from the air around us, from infancy. It's good to re-examine them against competing points of view we perceive in the course of living. We don't live on an island of neutrality, at any time, having no set of beliefs at all about the nature of reality. We have a baseline set of assumptions that we bring to the task of evaluating metaphysical propositions, but they sometimes go unacknowledged. It's quite possible to go through life not re-examining them at all. People sometimes do this because they falsely believe they hold to no truths about reality. They believe themselves perpetually open-minded. Sometimes agnostics are agnostics for this reason. One can become inured to the idea that he's neutral on the biggest question of God's existence, forgetting that the ultimate answer is all one way or the other, there's no in-between shade of gray.

This forgetting could be an instance of confusing belief with truth. If I believe there is no God, that doesn't mean there is no God. There either is or there isn't. The truth is independent of my belief. Truth and belief are two

CHAPTER 13: KNOWLEDGE, BELIEF, FAITH

distinct concepts. Likewise, if I believe there is a God, that doesn't mean there is a God. There is or there isn't, independent of what I believe.

This may all sound obvious, but people make exactly this mistake in their thinking all the time. It is among the reasons people wall themselves off from open-minded inquiry; why they invoke barriers to their own critical thinking, like reversing a burden of proof to place it on those who hold views in opposition to their own. When we're confronted with an alternative set of ideas about the nature of reality, we naturally examine them against what we already presume to be true, whether we're conscious of our existing beliefs or not. In this way, people delude themselves into thinking they evaluate ideas neutrally.

This is happening now in our overwhelmingly secular culture. Religion? Most people would say they're giving it a thumbs-up or thumbs-down on the merits. But if we give it a thumbs-down, what are we saying then about the nature of reality? Not "nothing," surely. It necessarily means an embrace of the anti-metaphysical proposition of materialism. But our culture doesn't lead us to a thumbs-up/thumbs-down evaluation of *that* proposition. Instead, we're left to falsely think of ourselves as neutral, rather than simply as materialists.

Attempting a misguided neutrality on metaphysical questions, like whether there is a God or not, can lead one to elevate materialism undeservedly to a position of presumptive correctness. With that perspective, materialism becomes the default explanation for all of reality, whether it is overtly adopted as such or not. Consequently, it can become habitual to assume that whatever about reality is not currently explained will eventually be explained in purely physical terms. This can mislead someone into a false neutrality on the most important of questions before us.

Chapter 14: **Significance**

THERE IS WITHIN EACH of us a desire for a lightness of existence, and likewise a desire for heaviness, or solidity. We are pulled in the direction of both, in our lives. One's self-perception is, among many other things, characterized as a mix of desire for *consequence*, in tension with a desire for *inconsequence*. Some people desire more than anything else a feeling of lightness of being; a feeling of freedom from the oppression of heavy, consequential, foreboding, omnipresent *Meaning*. Discussion of morals may be distasteful, not because one desires immorality, but because it implies that what they do matters. Living with a weight of significance feels like a constraint on freedom. People feel these things on a deep level, they don't think of weightiness and consequence as bad in themselves. They do, however, apprehend that they create tension pulling against their desire for freedom. They want personal autonomy, but not just that. They want an absence of consequence to any exercise of personal autonomy they may undertake. The more we emphasize purpose and meaning to life, the more we're conscious of a sense of consequence to what we do, and that may seem like a constraint to personal liberty.

At the same time, we fear the opposite: a complete absence of meaning. An absence of meaning and purpose in our lives unmoors us from a necessary sense of humanity. Nihilism first lures us by the promise of freedom, as we escape from the sense of heaviness, solidity, and consequence. It is meaning of life itself that we might find oppressive, and so we flee from it only to find the resulting lightness of being unbearable.* If we lay hold of meaninglessness, we lay hold of nihilism, and we're left to ask, with Albert Camus, whether that meaninglessness justifies suicide, or whether we're somehow saved merely by consciousness of the absurdity of our condition of meaninglessness.** Some purpose is necessary. Some meaning.

---

*This idea is reflected in the title of Milan Kundera's 1984 novel *The Unbearable Lightness of Being*.
**Camus, The Myth of Sisyphus (1942) opening lines.

CHAPTER 14: SIGNIFICANCE

There is nothing more weighty and consequential than God, if we rightly understand him and his relationship to us. It is deeply significant that man is made in the image of God. Christians sometimes refer to our inborn *imago Dei,* or refer to people as "image-bearers," to emphasize the elements of humanity that are held in common with God, including the orientations to truth and beauty and, especially, the ability to distinguish good from evil. We are made in the image of God because of this moral awareness and moral responsibility, combined with the scope of our conscious self-awareness, including the ability to perceive God from his creation, in this lifetime, and a continuing awareness thereafter.

Clearly, in all of creation there is no more significant relationship than that of the triune God to man. If we correctly perceive the omnipotence, omnibenevolence, and omniscience of God, and the astounding breadth and variety of his creation, and his timelessness compared to time-bound man, it is difficult to imagine that man is not elevated just by the association. And then to find that despite our rebellion, God accepts those who choose him, demonstrating in the process sacrificial love by One with no obligation to sacrifice, it is impossible not to see that man is supremely important to God. So much so that we must either blow it all off as being pure fancy and wishful thinking, or drop to our knees in humble gratitude to know we could ever be so important as this.

This significance of man to God must mean something in history, because God has revealed himself to mankind in the medium of history. If there is a God and if what we can know of him is true, he has developed mankind as a race for millennia, and it is an ongoing project. The relationship continues following the natural death of individual people. There is therefore a purpose to human lives. We are not admonished to live well and abundantly so that we'll be better off in life, or not for that reason only. There is a purpose to this relationship, only partly understood now. There is meaning to individual lives: to know God better and to serve him, meaning to advance his purposes and in the process serve ourselves, because in reality our interests are mutual.

We can regard God as being a far-off harrumphing scold on high, but if we do, we miss out. We find a semblance of purpose and meaning to life in abstractions and sloganeering, and maybe that's better than nothing, we're at least looking in the right direction. Better, though, to be united with Christ, the bridge to the Father, through a union that is spiritual and therefore closer than physical proximity in the body. In this way we find meaning and purpose to life; all that we can handle.

But that's Christianity. Perhaps Judaism, too, stripping this description of some of the specifics and regarding some of this as inchoate. A bit more of a stretch for Islam, but it, too, sees significance in mankind. What of the chief metaphysical view that competes with these monotheisms now in western culture? Is there meaning and purpose to materialism?

Well, in a word: no. In fact the absence of meaning and purpose is really the signal feature of materialism. It is founded on an explanation of mankind's provenance that explicitly disavows meaning. The whole point of naturalistic evolution, properly understood, is that mankind developed in the entire absence of any *telos*, or guiding principle or direction. Ancestor life forms did not evolve to mankind because mankind was a goal. There is no Being to have the goal, and human populations certainly don't act purposefully when environmental challenge results in deselection of poorer-surviving traits. There was no purpose to any step of the development, because there was no Being to purpose it. Purposelessness is the hallmark of mankind, in the materialist paradigm.

Now that doesn't make it false. We don't pick creation over naturalistic evolution just because we prefer to have purpose and creation supplies it. We don't pick the truth about how we got here at all. However it happened, it's the truth. Our fidelity to the truth orientation, above all else, demands that we not pragmatically pick and choose among the alternatives to appease our preferences.

But neither does the false conclusion of purposelessness imply that naturalistic evolution is true. It would seem more likely that if evolution is true at all, it is true through the operation of an inherent goal-directedness provided by God; that is, teleological evolution as opposed to passive, naturalistic evolution. This makes more sense on the science, and also given God's evident teleology in the history of the Jews, and the current interregnum following Christ's Ascension. Though the evidence seems slim, it's conceivable that God set evolution in place as a natural process and then adopted a resulting species, imbuing a line of hominids with his image and thereafter impressing his teleological ends upon that species' acts in history. It is also possible that our infatuation with evolution is misplaced; that the many criticisms of it are valid: irreducible complexity, absence of fossil record, absence of transitional types, taxonomical fluidity, and so on.

CHAPTER 14: SIGNIFICANCE

We don't know for sure. But we do know for sure that materialism is devoid of meaning or purpose for mankind, and if there is a God, our purpose lies in him. We also know there is a deep intuition of significance. That is not proof of God by itself, perhaps, but if it is not true then we have evolved the intuition of significance despite there being none.

Chapter 15: **Yearning**

IMAGINE YOU ARE ONE of those people who loves the outdoors, and not just in passing, buying a landscape calendar or driving past fall leaves, but one who sees a mountain range and wants to be in the middle of it, far from any road. Your desire is not just to be there. Your desire is to be in some sense at one with the mountain. At one with the mountain vegetation. At one with the interaction of plant and animal species that live there. At one with the thin atmosphere at altitude. You might feel a great sense of peace, coming off a weekend in one of those hallowed places. But it's never quite enough. You walk along mountain trails, maybe bushwhack through hardscrabble terrain, experience thirst and hunger and sunburn or oppressive shadow, but there is associated with it an almost spiritual quiet and healing. When you walk out of there, you may feel a little bit of let-down. It never quite feels complete. You were never really one with the mountains, you were just there, immersed in its grandness, for a time, but just there. You may recognize that your yearning is not merely to be there; not merely to exercise your body; not merely to exercise your mind trying to understand species of foliage and silvics and ecosystems. Your yearning really goes beyond all that. It was to *be* the mountain and its life and its atmosphere. That yearning is never fully satisfied just with a visit. And so you return, again and again, driven by yearning.

Yearning is the baseline experience of our lives.

"Yearning" refers to desire, but it carries with it the connotation of an emotional pull, a passion, that goes beyond merely wanting some material thing. I may thirst mightily for water, for example, but though I must have it or die, I wouldn't say my thirst constitutes a "yearning." I might say I "yearn" to be reunited with a loved one, however.

You may have a yearning for success in your profession, or to see your children thrive, or to walk along the beach at daybreak and feel continuity with the infinite-seeming space of the ocean, which stands in for eternity. In all these situations, the object of your yearning is not yet achieved. If you've

CHAPTER 15: YEARNING

succeeded well in your profession, and are nearing the end of your working days, the yearning for success may dissipate into a sense of satisfaction, or be replaced with a more modest and realistic kind of yearning. The vocational yearning, while it burned within you, drove you to whatever success you did achieve. Perhaps your chosen profession was the rearing of your own small children, and now they're grown. You still want them to thrive, of course, but the yearning gives way to satisfaction. Or resignation.

For all of us the yearning is relatively inchoate, in youth, when all things are possible, but becomes more acute, as we approach middle age, and especially as we find some of our yearning frustrated. No matter our age, however, there is yearning. The yearning we feel is never fully satisfied, really. Frustration of our yearning, to one degree or another, is a natural condition. Past a certain age, no one alive is without some disappointment. Disappointment can be sublimated as a driver to other healthy ambitions, and that is the right way to deal with it. It is a part of the disorder of the world, a part of the sense that things are in some way broken. We feel a desire all throughout our lives for something we don't have, and it drives us, in good ways and bad. Frustration and disappointment signal the presence of this yearning. What is its nature? Where does it come from? What does it tell us about who we are?

It's certainly easy enough to settle into a season of watching TV, plugging into an alternative "reality" for a period that eats up big parts of our life, followed each day by rising up to trudge off dutifully to work, repeating the cycle countless times. But that is a tamping-down of the burbling yearning metabolism of our lives. Teenage children are frustrated with their parents in part because of their own nascent frustrations of this yearning, but also because of their vicarious frustration at their parents' misguided squelching of life. This yearning is not there to be roped and bridled and brought to heel, dragging it down and subjugating it to fear-formed zones of safety, even if the culture seems to approve it. If Christianity is true, we are to be lifted out of all this. We should be feeding and growing our yearning. It is our bean-stalk connection to God. Instead of cultivating it, we live in fear, keeping this yearning in half-light in the basement, clipping it back and starving it of nutrients, embarrassed that it exists at all.

We should recognize that the yearnings we feel have no basis in materialism, but they have independent meaning if our intuition of God's existence is true. Not only is this intuition reliable unto itself, but it means we can attach meaning to the sense of yearning we all feel for that which we can but dimly perceive. That yearning points us to something higher, to a possible fulfillment of that yearning in God's love.

A fairly obvious kind of yearning in most people is the yearning for a mate. If you're a young unmarried person, pay heed. That subtle, muffled note of alarm you sense may only be political correctness telling you to raise your sensitivity antenna, as if admitting to this particular kind of yearning represents an affront to the personal autonomy we're supposed to cherish and cultivate. It's ok, it's just you and me here. Perhaps you've not experienced a desire for a husband or wife, particularly. Maybe there's not a strong desire for children, or you attach little importance to the traditional family model as the context for rearing them. Or maybe the marriage estate strikes you as a bit bourgeois and unnecessary; one of those limitations on freedom that you feel should not be expected of you. You might find the idea a bit cloying, because it's a lifetime proposition, in theory. But very likely you've had some feeling of interest in being twined with someone else, if only for a season. Something in the psyche is touched by the special interest of another, and it's not merely gratification of ego, because the feelings are reciprocated. It is not an interest that is several among others, but rather is unique to one. It invites a vulnerability that we don't expose for just anyone. This is why break-ups are hard.

The yearning is for someone with whom to share life. Preferably someone who is not your clone, in personality, so that he or she brings a freshness to the shared living. He or she might have something you lack, in fact. If you're an introvert, perhaps you're attracted to an extrovert. If you're heavily analytical, perhaps you feel drawn to share life with someone of a more lyrical disposition. The person you share life with—real and now or imagined for the future—is the Other in your life, one with whom you are mentally joined in a way that the grafting together feels natural, producing an intuitively satisfying new platform upon which to build your life.

Among the differences between you and that Other are those inherent in masculinity and femininity. These are not amenable to succinct definition, they're more *know-it-when-you-see-it* qualities. Sometimes we have to look past caricatures of masculine and feminine, to see the real thing underneath. But always we're looking at our perception of those qualities in the Other: masculine responding to feminine and vice versa.

The very existence of this draw proves the fact of yearning in general, and of yearning for life-partner in particular. What does this tell us? According to Christianity, it tells us that this liaison between a particular man and particular woman, and even its permanent nature, is of God. God created mankind, and as the Bible prominently emphasizes, "male and female he created them." Masculine and feminine both originated in the mind and creative power of God. Masculinity and femininity separated out within mankind at creation.

Obviously these qualities are not absolute in the sexes. Individual men may be less masculine than an aspirational ideal, or may turn it into a laughable undisciplined counterfeit. Individual women may be less feminine than an aspirational ideal, or may distort true femininity by indulging their worst instincts. On top of these elements of mankind's disordered state, there seems to be a perennial debate, inwardly and outwardly, about what it even means to be masculine and feminine. It's worth finding out and cultivating, because it matters to God. We read passages on this subject in the Bible that seem strange to modern ears, but made perfect sense until the day before yesterday. Injunctions against wearing the clothes of the opposite sex, for example. Why would that matter? The idea is that striving for the ideals of one's sex is to be preserved, it is a noble and right thing to do. It is a positive movement, individually and as a society, toward the wholeness of combined masculine and feminine, signifying our ability to draw closer to the pre-sex-differentiated wholeness of God. We don't accomplish it individually, by trying to combine both masculine and feminine traits within us. Instead we're to look outward for the opposite in another. Our survival as a race down through the generations even depends on it. This is a part of the significance of God's having made us male and female.

There is a significant time element to this, too, in that God is timeless and unchanging, so this union between man and woman is to be permanent (in this life) too. The importance of this is the more obvious when we consider the emotional need of children for this unchanging foundation for their world. It is necessary to their development, including their development of ideals of masculine and feminine. People sometimes have to live in less than ideal circumstances, such as single parenthood, and as with anything else in this disordered world, we make the best of it we can. Or a couple might marry but remain childless, so that this consideration seems less pressing, but a childless family is not an exception to the larger purposes for marriage. We should not lose sight of the ideal. Children are the way in which mankind is immortal, in the flesh. The family is the support system for a child, and is therefore the irreducible element of mankind's immortality in the flesh. We live on in the generations that follow, and we are connected generationally back in time to creation.

There is a lot of spiritual mystery packed into marriage, for the theist. There is the aisle that the bride walks down, a re-creation of the blood covenant of God with His people through Abraham. The father gives the bride away, not because he owns her or because the woman has no independent self, but rather because she occupies a unique place, in this union: an ark of the generations following, as Mary was the ark of Jesus, as God's presence was manifested in the ark of the covenant, as mankind was salvaged in the ark of Noah. She symbolizes too the church, for whose redemption God in the person of Jesus willingly laid down the life he lived in the body, feeling all the pain and betrayal and abandonment that those of us in the flesh can be made to feel, plus abandonment of the Father and interruption of the love relationship more complete than we are able to discern. The picture of Christ in relation to the church presents an aspirational level of commitment by the groom to his bride. The contributions of male and female to the marriage estate are different in kind, not amenable to a simplistic vision of equality at the expense of love. There is a spiritual element to the marriage union that distinguishes mere life-partnership.

The sex drive may be strong, but female companionship to a man, and male companionship to a female, is more fundamental to our humanity. The sex drive can be expressed in seemingly inconsequential transactions, rather than be sublimated to its greater meaning, as we all, on some level, really desire. For a man, when sex is over, the unmatured instinct may be to return to one's male companions, or solitude. But there's something deeper involved, a yearning that is not met by degrading faceless hook-ups. A man is missing out, when he has sex and then immediately moves on, and he knows it. A woman typically knows it even better, but she, like a man, can be hardened to this as a reality. The sex drive is so powerful that it can obscure the more significant drivers behind it, like small breaking waves might obscure the tsunami that lifts them all. A man doesn't just want a mechanical release, though he may, unfortunately, settle for that. The physical tension exists because he desires a woman. And though he may transactionally take a woman to meet the wavelet of his urges, it doesn't suffice for the tsunami of his real need. Women tend to be more oriented to the underlying tsunami, but understand the wavelets, too, sometimes using them for short-term purposes, separating them from the larger yearning that underlies them. This requires stripping the sex act from the mutual

CHAPTER 15: YEARNING

knowing and consequent love that it represents. For both men and women, the sex drive is a form of yearning, best fulfilled in marriage. And yet we should be careful in our estimation of the marriage estate not to consider it superior. Singleness is our default position, and if we marry, we should do so cautiously, "advisedly," as older marriage messages used to warn, precisely because marriage is so weighted with metaphysical meaning.

But what if there were no God? What would the evidence of marriage tell us then? It seems there is a permanent or at least long-term pairing off even among people who reject God. It could be that the idea of marriage is a hold-over from formerly Christian culture, but it could also be that sexual forbearance and then monogamy are among the foundational moral principles of individual conscience, felt instinctively. We should ask what a Godless universe would mean to marriage. Marriage, if it's instinctive, would have to have evolved as a societal norm in order to enhance survivability, as an element of the social nature of human beings and success of progeny. As such, it suffers from the same problem as other instincts we assign the word "moral" to. They didn't come about because they're authoritative. They didn't come about because they are in some way true. They came about because they made an individual more fit for survival. Realizing this, why obey the instinct? Our reason is at least as authoritative as animal instinct formed for purposes no longer applicable.

Chapter 16: **Beauty**

LET'S RECALIBRATE OUR PURPOSES, slightly, to the question whether materialism is a true understanding of reality, or whether there is a God; and if there is a God, is he the God to which Christianity points? To try to answer these, we're looking at bits of evidence, and considering them in light of a theist or Christian understanding, and in light of materialism. So next let's consider beauty. As with the discussions here about truth and about morality, we're not talking about whether this or that is beautiful or not. We're considering beauty in the abstract; whether the fact that we perceive beauty is evidence on these questions we pursue.

Beauty is as much a base-line orientation for human beings as is truth. As with truth, we can think of the desire for beauty as part of the operating system of our lives. "Beauty" doesn't just mean attractive people. It also means the color symphony of fall leaves, and the mysterious call of mountain ranges fading into the far distance, and sunsets over the ocean, garish and glorious. These are visual, but beauty may also inhere in other sense impressions, such as with music or even cuisine. Well-composed and intellectually gratifying literature works almost entirely within the intellect, but can be beautiful like other types of beauty presenting as sense impressions.

Beauty is aligned with our perception of order in the world. Order is aligned with our perception of meaningfulness. The opposite of beauty is found in the discordant, the chaotic, and the meaningless. Beauty most fundamentally points us to the true, the purposeful, the meaningful, the significant, and the transcendent. We regard an experience of beauty as being "transcendent" because in our minds it takes us to an appreciation for something beyond the fact of our plain, brute existence, to an intimation of something in and through that existence but also beyond it, to a meaningfulness and significance that goes beyond our physical lives and surroundings. Through beauty we touch spiritual truth.

Our every thought is channeled toward the good, the true, and the beautiful in the same way that it is channeled by time. If naturalistic

CHAPTER 16: BEAUTY

biological evolution is thought to be the paradigm for matter-over-mind naturalism, it's easy to chalk up beauty to survivability. Doesn't a woman's beauty enhance her own survival and the likelihood of progeny? But think of beauty in a more abstract way. Instead of sexual attraction, think of a time when you were transported by music. Perhaps swelling, uplifting worship music, or even popular secular music that "strikes a chord," as we say, because it seems to resonate harmoniously within us. It may affect us at such a deep level that it seems to raise our consciousness of self; our self-awareness as a human being among other human beings, together under the dome of heaven united rather than separated, uncluttered by atomizing differences that distract and seem to harass us. Think of a mountain path that curves ahead of you beguilingly so that you don't see to the end of it, and imagine late afternoon light flooding in and creating shadowed contrasts with every natural color imaginable, as though filtered through the finest stained glass in a vaulted cathedral with ceilings so high they disappear into the empyrean. Why does this make us think of God?

Imagine you're standing at the foot of snow-clad mountains, majestic in the glow of ethereal early-morning light. You feel something. It induces emotion, it's not just observation of angles, lines, color, lighting. You're "uplifted." You're recharged. You feel renewed, as if your place in the world is somehow validated. You may even feel a sense of gratitude, or humility, or perhaps you feel small and enlarged at the same time: small compared to the majesty of that mountain view; large in contemplating the depth and complexity of your sentient, self-aware being alongside that unspeaking mountain. We may think of this as a moment of transcendence. We're experiencing something beyond the brute facts of rock, snow, atmosphere. That beauty and that feeling it induces in us are not just emergent properties of our physical processes and of the mountainscape. There is in fact something beyond. We feel "transcendence" because we sense that something indeed transcends the physical composition in front of us. We are drawn out of ourselves, so to speak, toward that something higher. That's the impact of beauty on us.

Once we begin to think of beauty as a hard proof of God, along with truth and goodness, we begin to separate its heart-pull from the greater reality to which it points. If there were nothing higher toward which to be drawn, would we experience beauty at all? One could attempt to argue that man's biological evolution gives him an inward orientation toward beautiful people, places, food, music, and so on, but it's a tough sell. The reason is that one would have to truncate the very thing that makes it beautiful in the first place: that sense of transcendence; that the object of admiration points to something deeper and more meaningful than the thing unto itself.

Indeed, if evolution were the sole explanation for beauty, then we would be appreciating some things more than others, attaching the label "beautiful," only because those more beautiful things enhance our survivability. But our appreciation of beauty is not correlated to survivability, apart from sexual attraction. Functionality is distinct from beauty. That's not to say that a functional item like a well-crafted table may not be beautiful, but if so it is beautiful for reasons apart from its utility. More conventional instances of beauty—paintings, music, flower arrangements—have no utilitarian or survival value at all. In fact, we ascribe beauty more readily to that which has no utilitarian value precisely because it has no utilitarian value; because its only purpose is beauty. As such, it unambiguously gratifies our longing for the transcendent, spiritual, reality to which the beauty points, more obviously than if its purpose is mingled with practical physical purposes.

Beauty should be understood as entirely perplexing to the materialist vision of reality. If there were no reality which transcends our physical existence, it is doubtful we would experience beauty at all. All of existence would be flat. Our emotions would be useless, atrophied or never emergent in the first place. Concepts like dignity, honor, virtue, courage, valor, purity, even love, would lose meaning altogether. We would just be complex collections of carbon-based compounds, moving through our environment processing elements of that environment until the process ceases and those elements return inert to the environment. There would be no sense of high and low at all, and no feeling of transcendence because there would not be, in fact, anything which transcends this material existence.

Chapter 17: **Gratitude**

WE MODERNS ARE OBSESSED with "happiness," perhaps because it seems ever more elusive. It is elusive if we no longer conceive of it as harmony with a real God. We tend to think of it as something like contentment. A close cousin of contentment is resignation, however, and certainly happiness means more than that. Nor is it another extreme from contentment: a kind of deluded narcotic unreality. It's not exhilaration or giddiness. Happiness is a feeling, but it's a feeling difficult to reduce to words beyond contentment or satisfaction or equanimity. We hardly know what happiness is, yet we are always pursuing it. It's one of those things we only see when not looking directly at it. We know happiness by what it's *not*: anxiety, unrest, fear, uncertainty.

Studies about happiness usually involve correlating expressions of subjective feelings of happiness to variables like physical health, financial wealth, strength of relationships, or personality traits. One very common positive correlation is that between happiness and gratitude. Dictionary definitions of gratitude often loop back on themselves, as with "the quality of being grateful." Part of the reason for this tendency to self-reference is that the word has no meaning except in reference to something else. We know it means being appreciative, thankful, and grateful. But *to whom*?

We could suppose that it is other people. Who would not be grateful to their parents, for example, if they were loved and well cared-for in childhood? How churlish not to be. But if, as good materialists, we consider that our parents, like we ourselves, only behave in the way they do because of the innumerable influences upon them from their respective pasts, then why be grateful? They were just doing what their genes dictated. Our care for others is the product of mindless, directionless, biological impulses, in turn derived from purposeless, directionless evolution. Our parents weren't behaving in a way for which they deserve our thanks. They were behaving in the way their biology directed them. Love is not a thing they shared in and in turn shared with us. Love is just a fuzzy word we attach to nice feelings we get with some people. They're just feelings that our biology engenders to advance our survival imperatives. Giving thanks would seem to be a perplexing concept for one who rejects God.

The idea of gratitude—motivating thanks-giving—is closely tied to humility. We don't thank ourselves, after all. We recognize that what we are and who we are and what we have are attributable to something outside ourselves. A person who believes that the material universe is all there is could certainly say he is the product of forces outside of himself, just as can the theist. So perhaps the materialist could have the gratitude that would motivate him to thanks-giving too?

We could suppose that a materialist would have a sense of humility, because man is not self-made, after all. Even a materialist would think of forces of the universe having operated so that they culminate in this person in this moment of reflection, contemplating that but for those forces, he would not be here to experience gratitude. The materialist might contemplate the awesome majesty and mystery of the material mechanisms that operated to bring him into being. We are composed of stardust, after all!

But those forces are mindless, unguided, and purposeless. The materialist would have to consider himself purely an accident. There is no softer spin to put on it, because the materialist point of view is that there was no single driving force that had man as its object. Man is not a "creation," even if we use the word while excluding the possibility of a sentient creator, because the *purpose* of creating mankind is missing. There is no one before whom to have humility. This emotion of humility concerning one's own existence is wasted, if we live in a purely naturalistic reality.

We are grateful for the love and time and attention and things that are given to us precisely because we did not generate those things for ourselves. In the case of love, or the feeling behind gifts, or the teaching, or the instilling of discipline, these are things we are grateful for in part because they cannot be self-generated. We get these things from others because we are incapable of developing them on our own. You can have self-discipline, but someone else has to demonstrate self-discipline to you. You can have learning, but someone must teach you. You can love, but someone must first show you love. We may be grateful for what we get, but what makes us grateful is the fact that it comes from someone else rather than being something we generate on our own. To place ourselves in a position to be taught, or to love, means showing humility—the humility of receiving.

CHAPTER 17: GRATITUDE

We generally think humility is a positive character trait. It is how a person feels and demonstrates self-awareness that the superlative of every good quality does not rest with him. But why would we consider humility a virtue if we hold to materialism? Humility, and therefore a sense of gratitude, is evidence that we are created beings, and so the origin of all humility is humility before our Creator. Likewise with gratitude. The origin of all gratitude is gratitude for that creation, and again, it is expressed to our Creator. We feel humility and gratitude in our daily lives, and celebrate these as virtues, because there is a God. If there weren't, they would make no sense.

Chapter 18: **Religion**

Doctrine vs. Rites and Practices

To consider religion as evidence we must first reduce it to its essence. Our question initially is not whether this set of doctrines or that is true; it is whether the fact of religion tells us something about whether there is a God or not, or whether naturalism fully explains reality. The essence of religion, for our purposes, is a set of doctrines concerning supernatural reality, to which a community of believers subscribes.

It's tempting to oversimplify religion as being only about rites and practices. John Dewey, in the first half of the twentieth century, saw it that way, and strove to develop a secular society composed of religion-like rites and practices, starting with the public schools. It should be obvious, however, that the point of religious practice is to acknowledge a deity or deities, and the particular rites and practices followed would relate to doctrines concerning the deity. Rites and practices by themselves by no means explain religion. Religions do involve organized, communal shared activities, but that's not the real point. The communal nature of religious practice reflects some religious tenets, but is not by itself a sufficient explanation of religion. Theology defines religion. It is not merely social gathering institutionalized.

Suppose you wanted to understand why religious congregations behave the way they do. You could buy a book that identifies the way they congregate and the types of dress and mannerisms and motions gone through during a typical worship service. It would be a pretty unsatisfying book if it did not explain those matters on the basis of theological differences. The point is that though rites and practices and the particular communal feature of various religions reflect differing theological beliefs, they are not the essence of what religion is. The essence of religion is the theological doctrines to which religious congregants subscribe. Chief among those doctrines will be doctrines concerning the nature of God, or of particular gods, or of divine essence in some other form.

CHAPTER 18: RELIGION

Religions generally presuppose the existence of a reality beyond the natural world. They may differ as to what that extra-physical reality is, but it is significant that there are so many people who hold to supernatural belief. (To be complete, there are some religions which do not speak to the existence of the divine at all, and are properly regarded as "lifestyle" religions which would not figure into the phenomenon of the near-ubiquity of human belief in something beyond the physical world.) That religion is so generally a feature of human civilization down through the ages suggests it exists because of a God-oriented instinct in people, which in turn suggests that God is.

Some would argue the opposite inference, however, because religions are so diverse. The argument would be that the religious impulse evidences some feature of the human psyche evolved to induce credulity about a putative deity, perhaps to advance survival through social living, rather than constituting evidence that the object of the religious impulse is real. Some atheists assert their agreement with Christianity in disbelieving all the gods of all the other religions; they just add one more to their pantheon of disbelief, throwing out the putative Christian God as well.

One among several problems with this approach is that it implicitly puts the atheist in a position of neutrality concerning metaphysical questions, but that is a position that does not exist. The materialist outlook on metaphysics is just as significant as the various religions' outlook on metaphysics. We should re-arrange our categories, if we're going to take this argument seriously. It's not as though there are all the religions arrayed on one side of the question, and materialism on the other. The various religions are comprised of various views of metaphysics. Materialism is another view of metaphysics. The relevant category is all metaphysical views, not theistic metaphysical views.

On this understanding, materialism does not get special privilege. It is true or not true in the same way that other metaphysical views are true or not true. Just because monotheisms and pantheisms disagree about the nature of God does not mean he doesn't exist. Put the shoe on the other foot, for a moment. Would we say that because materialists disagree with pantheists, Christianity must be true?

God gave us the reason and intuition that impel us toward him. He also made us time-bound mortals, in this life, so we don't presently have a complete window into his kingdom whereby we can more fully understand him. Clearly, he is not like us. And so we come to understanding of his nature as best we can through revelation and reason, and the social aspect of our consciousness leads us to do so communally, adopting over time carefully-crafted doctrines that we believe accurately describe God and his relationship to us. We seek a "systematic" theology precisely because we expect our resulting belief to be supported by reason. That effort has not yielded uniformity of opinion—to put it mildly—about principles of theology, for a number of reasons that can be summarized as the fact that we are not-God, groping after the ineffable.

All religions cannot be true, because they make inconsistent and sometimes mutually exclusive claims about the nature of God. So some sets of religious belief must be wrong. More probably all are, at least in relatively trivial ways, because we're talking here about mere human understanding about almighty God. The fact that there are religions that get it wrong on major points or minor ones does not mean there is no God. Nor does the fact of a diversity of metaphysical views mean the anti-metaphysical view is right.

The Necessity of God

In early Western civilization there was a sense that God was necessary to explain the existence of ourselves and everything we see around us. While pagan gods of various kinds were honored so as to keep life in harmony, it was thought there had to be some overarching creative force of some kind that would explain the existence of the material world. People intuited that the world and the cosmos could not have created itself.

Coming at the same point from a different direction, the God necessary as the Creator to creation was also seen as the transcendent ideal of perfect states, as with Plato's forms, or of ultimate purpose, as with the teleology of Aristotle, and morally as the perfection to which we might aspire but never quite reach: "that than which nothing greater exists," in St. Anselm's formulation, though the idea long pre-dated him.

Kierkegaard alluded to the idea that a system cannot include the systematizer, in the context of demonstrating that a purportedly complete philosophical system could not be complete if there is an "outside" to it. The Bible at Romans 1:20 reads: "For [God's] invisible attributes, namely, his eternal power and divine nature, have been clearly perceived, ever since the creation of the world, in the things that have been made. . . ." This sounds like high-minded flowing poetry, but it's also literally true. It is essentially a statement that the existence of material reality is proof of the immaterial reality beyond it. Material things cannot spring from true nothing without some immaterial outside agency.

If you're a materialist philosopher of causation you might say that everything we observe is contingently caused, meaning that there is a combination of material and forces acting upon the material which explains everything that is or that happens. Everything is "contingent" on preceding causes. If we're to trace it back to a non-contingent first cause, which we must do if nature is all there is, we hop on a moving sidewalk that goes backward forever, in an infinite regress. Logic tells us there had to be a beginning to the chain of causation. There had to be some cause that was not itself caused.

The uncaused cause has to lie outside the reality of contingent causes. Aristotle was right about the concept of pure actuality standing apart from all the potentialities that proceed from it. What "calls into being that which does not exist" (Romans 4:17) is God. When Moses wrote that God is the great "I Am" (Exodus 3:14) and Jesus echoed these words about himself (John 8:58), they were making an ontologically sound philosophical statement. God's existence necessarily precedes and effectuates the material reality we know.

The Personal Nature of God

So there's a God, but should we understand this entity to be "God"—in quote marks, instead? That is, should we regard the originating uncaused-cause to be some sort of poorly-understood creative force so beyond humanity that he is unrecognizable to us? Or are we to view him as an extrapolation backward of the uniqueness of human beings—the reverse of our idea that we are made in his image? That is, can we say that he is in some way like us because we know that we are a little bit like him? Is he something more personal than amorphous creative force?

The first conception would make of God a sort of avatar, a label to attach to a bound-together collection of philosophical necessities. A popular modern commentator, Jordan Peterson, seems to hold to this sort of formulation of "God," at least as of the date of this writing.

Alternatively, we might regard God as being a personal God, in the sense of having what we regard as human-like attributes. We experience subjectively an evaluation of positive traits in other people all the time, and while we certainly do not on each such occasion acknowledge it as being a reflection of the goodness of God, rather than emanating from the person himself, we can't help but have mankind in mind, when we raise our eyes to look upon God. It takes some imagination to understand those traits originating in their unsullied purity from on high; "imagination" in the sense of developing the mental "image" of the ideals though we ourselves contain only dull reflections of them.

He is a personal God if he cares about our most intimate comings and goings and doings. This makes sense if we consider the moral dimension of God as opposed to his creative force or the order and beauty of his creation. He is, after all, the ultimate judge. He doesn't merely sit on high and pass judgment on this act or that one—though he does that, too—more fundamentally, he embodies justice. He is purely just and wholly right, but he's not merely at an extreme on a sliding scale of justness. He is the scale. He defines justice and righteousness. Just as he is pure actuality and the sole uncaused-cause, so he is the only One who is justice itself.

Hell

Those of us made in his image are contingent beings, coming into existence through the agency of our parents, who, like us, are not-God. By virtue of our not-God-ness we stand in opposition to the judge of our souls because it is our nature to do so. We make God our enemy and he is right to remove us from the family of beings bearing his image, the image stamped on us in the form of shared consciousness, moral agency, and an understanding of truth, beauty, and goodness as ideals we are to make it our business to pursue.

This removal is to hell. In our culture people laugh off the idea of hell, but only because it is poorly understood. It's not necessarily a place, because we're talking about a spiritual reality outside the constraints of physical things. We choose hell when we repudiate God as the Absolute, and the means of reconciliation he provides. We have moral agency, which means we have responsibility for what we do. Just as we have the ability to choose a proper relationship to God, we have the ability to reject him. God does not send us to hell, but he does remove his presence if that's what we want, and the result is hell. All the good things about this life are from God, and all the bad things are what exist in the shadows, places we have the moral agency to keep from him and which are therefore not irradiated by him. If we reject the light, all is shadow. As always, we choose, and God honors our choice.

Even if it is our choice, we could look on this as harsh, perhaps unfair, even. To make this conclusion, though, we have to mentally set aside the God's-image attributes of our humanity. We have to imagine ourselves as animals, without the moral imperatives and truth orientation, and consciousness individually and socially, and the experience of transcendence in the face of beauty, including the awesomeness of the ordered creation we are privileged to delve into with the rationality and intellectual scope given us as image-bearers of God. If we're to have no consequence for our choice to repudiate God and these gifts, then "fairness" dictates we don't have those benefits, either.

It is in the nature of the gifts themselves that they come with the price tag of moral responsibility. We can't repudiate the lows but accept the highs. You might say we didn't choose to be image-bearers, and thus did not choose to have the moral awareness along with the moral responsibility that go with that estate. True enough, but neither do tigers choose their tiger-ness, nor lilies their lily-ness. Before I exist, there is no "me" to do the choosing. We're here. We are what we are. What are we going to do with it? Embrace the wholeness and the specialness to which we are called? Or remain deluded in our ignorance and petulance, descending to nihilism in this life and hell in the next?

Love and Justice

Love is evidence of ultimate reality. We can think of God as only a God of justice, but the evidence tells us that can't be so. His justice must co-exist with his love. It is for us to work out how these two things go together. If we do, we'll see that they *necessarily* go together. Unless they are joined in the character of God, we unravel in one direction or the other. If God loves us but demands nothing of us morally, then we are diminished; not recognizably human. If God judges us but does not love us, we have no hope for redemption. These alternatives each describe relationships without the real love or true justice we actually know. The tension between God's justice and love are resolved in the Savior, God's provision of the means of our reconciliation to him.

We become confused because we're forever imagining God to be like us, and so we have a hard time imagining a God of both perfect justice and perfect love. We miss the mark about this idea of proper fear of the Lord because we wonder: How can a God whom we're to fear because of our trespasses also sacrifice himself for us? No human judge is going to overlook our trespasses, and certainly no human judge has the power or inclination to sacrifice himself in order to do so. We are given the beginning of an understanding of how God can do so, however, in the Trinity.

In his book *The Story of Reality* (2017), Gregory Koukl provides an unusually clear statement of Christianity in contrast to the competing belief systems currently prevailing. He writes of Jesus that he came "to rescue us from the Father."* This doesn't sit well with people who haven't fully worked it all out, but it's exactly right. God is justice. God is love. The two aren't in conflict, in fact they necessarily go together. Hell is not an example of God's love. It's an instance of His justice. His love is manifested in his offer of pardon from hell. Many decline the offer of love, but they can't decline His justice. God cannot be not-God like we are.

To speak further of love, we must think about what love is, and what it isn't. Romantic love is exciting, but it is by no means the full manifestation of love. Romantic love is to love as spindrift is to the ocean. Love takes many forms, and we tend to think of each as its own phenomenon. We have this one word "love," and we need the word to encompass all the more particular kinds of love, but if we don't have the words for the various particulars, we have to make do with qualifiers, such as "romantic love" rather than just "love." And in truth, we don't have enough qualifiers. We should consider love in all its manifestations and in all its breadth: as a sense of fellow-feeling with every person we encounter; as intergenerational mentorship; as filial affection twined with respect; as sibling bonds that cannot be sundered despite meeting none of the expectations of friendship; as that special unstated understanding with a "best friend;" as help-meet and companion of one of the opposite sex; and as compassion, especially when expressed to unlovely and difficult people. And countless hues and intensities in-between.

One more: the love of man for God. It comes of recognition that any love in man originated with God. Theologians sometimes say that relationally receiving and in turn giving love is ontologically significant for mankind: it is what we are. The most basic way in which mankind is made in the image of God is the sharing of love. Love is not diminished when shared, but is enhanced, and people can thus direct love back

---

*Koukl, Story of Reality, p. 117.

to God without giving any of it up. This love is expressed in worship; or "worth-ship," our expression of that which is most important to us. It is also expressed in our conscious effort to understand what God wants of us, and doing it. It is expressed in sacrifice, which we are to understand is, at its most fundamental level, relinquishing a present right in something now, for a better return later, and finding ourselves both now and later enriched. It is the expansion of the time horizon, making us wise. It is the willingness to order our present life for the impact it has on the next. It is faith, by which we continually re-affirm the truth of that which is unseen, despite its being unseen. It is prayer, by which we invoke God's mercy and continually re-align ourselves with him. And it is community, by which the culture of human-to-human shared consciousness is centered upon God. This last is why church is important to Christians.

If we lump all these kinds of love together, and consider love in the abstract, like a flow of honey in and through the world of human beings, we can more easily conceive of love as a thing which is difficult to explain in the absence of God, its originator. Love is beyond comprehension unless there is a greater Love behind it all. Evil in the world is not the difficult thing to explain. Love is. As human beings we know love and we attach truth to love, not to airy abstractions and not to institutions.

Love According to Materialism

We know the love of God because we understand relational giving and receiving of human love and we come to understand there is a Source of that love placed in us. If there is no Being who is a Source of that love, then we are left to find an explanation for it in materialism. Materialism holds that there is no Author of love, but rather only ground-up biological development which includes the various phenomena we call "love." There is no one source of love at all, but only emotional properties emergent from evolution. It is thought to come from millions of years of deselection of traits we label less loving, as a result of environmental pressures on populations of human beings and their evolutionary ancestors. The urge to survive and procreate (wherever that comes from) is enhanced by social living, which is enhanced by feelings we describe by some variant of the word "love."

Thus, that feeling you have for your offspring is instinct rooted in biology, it has no existence outside the interplay of particular chemicals and tissues in your body. The same is true for your "love" felt toward a sibling, a friend, a potential mate, or toward mankind in the abstract, expressed as altruism, or what used to be called charity. In this vision, we are living out our biological imperatives, and the feeling we call "love" is just one among them, so it's time to throw out the word "love," or else rid it of all its sentimental connotations of enchantment.

The curious thing is that love doesn't feel like it's only a matter of biological instinct. It feels as if we choose love, especially when we choose love in the face of hatred and fear directed at us (as Jesus the Christ did). Love can only come from one of two sources. Either it's an internal instinct worked out in our thoughts and actions; or it's an ontological condition of our existence, a phenomenon in which we live and move and have our being, sourced outside ourselves but flowing into us and then again out of us to other people.

We all know of people who did not know love and therefore have little to give; and also of people who did not know love yet manage to express it to others. Love comes into our lives from the outside, and it projects from us toward others. The better evidence is that love has an external source, and that the ultimate source is outside mankind altogether, manifested in love from our Creator.

Love for God is love by instinct—instinct placed by God—for all that is good and true and beautiful, recognizing that there has to be an Author for those things, and then developing a desire to know that Author because this enchantment animating our life makes life good and worthwhile. Life is materially hard, for many people. And yet, their happiness is determined by the presence or absence of love in their life, not by the presence or absence of material prosperity. This is a familiar movie plot-line, but it's familiar because it is so manifestly true. Love is not just an evolved play of chemicals in the body to encourage social living, procreation, and rearing of children. Love is more than a bottom-up emergent property of meat machines that convince themselves they have a "self" consisting of more than just physical processes. Love is a top-down manifestation of the God who authors it, and whose very essence is love.

Love seems to be a phenomenon that is ever replenished. People die, but we don't think of their love as dying with them. We know, as we stand at the grave-side, that it lives on in us. Love never seems to be depleted. In some way we cannot presently fully understand, God re-energizes the world with love, from generation to generation, and his love in that way sustains the world. He infuses it with love and for that reason it does not rot from within as a result of the evil that mankind expresses so naturally.

Love as the Nature of God

The fact of love tells us something about the personal nature of God. A God who cares what we do because of his just nature is one thing; a God who cares what we do because of his love for us is something else altogether. The twin features of God's essence in relationship to us—justice and love—prove His personal nature. He is not merely the far-off creator of deist conception, but One we can picture being active in the world, though we may not understand exactly how.

The perspective we have now is subjective, which means we necessarily evaluate ideas about God within the medium of our conscious thought, rather than as a pure abstraction. The subjective consideration of the nature of God takes place inside the limited minds of people—at this moment, for example, mine and yours. So the conception of God is going to be limited by the capacity of those doing the conceiving, except insofar as the ability is expanded by God himself. It is likely quite literally true that the fear of the Lord is the beginning of wisdom;* it is not merely a restatement of the proposition that those who are wise acknowledge and revere God. There has to be some sense in which the consciousness of God interacts with the consciousness of those who choose him, opening our minds to the source of love and the truths he embodies. It also makes sense that this activity would be manifested most actively in prayer.

This is important because prayer, according to the Bible, is essential in our relationship to God, but it wouldn't be if God were not active in the world in some way; if he did not respond to us in some way, intervening in space-time because of fervent beseeching by those who trust that he is, and that his character is as the Bible reveals. Prayer, or rather its importance in the Christian paradigm of our relationship to God, is additional significant evidence that God is not impersonal. It is evidence that stands alongside the presence of love in the world, and the fact that human beings also carry the image of God in the fact of their moral awareness.

*Proverbs 9:10.

Savior

Preceding sections are about the love of God, which is a natural introduction to the idea of a Savior as the means of reconciliation to God, though he is just and we are not. Jesus, the Christ, is the means by which God's justice is tempered by his mercy, and he is the proof of the special relationship God has to mankind. You probably know the basic story-line. Jesus was foretold in Jewish scriptures going back thousands of years. He is written in vignettes throughout the Old Testament unmistakably. If you knew nothing of Christ but read the Old Testament you'd find it to be pointing to a momentous Messianic event of God yet to come. It is a curious combination of stories, some of which don't seem to have any connection to anything else, other than the common theme of a future redeemer, until you read the New Testament. If you're privileged to have come at the New Testament only after having a fairly thorough knowledge of the Old, you might be surprised. You might find yourself suddenly reaching back to the Old with understanding as to why it contains the particular stories it does, and not others. You might find yourself shocked to realize that the stories of the Old Testament foretell Christ in all the particulars of the life of Jesus. You might come to realize that the Old Testament could not possibly have been written the way it was, unless Jesus was the culmination of the Jews' history to the date of Christ's Ascension. The events of Jesus's life, death, and resurrection can't be swept aside as a creative add-on to Hebrew history.

Of course, that all assumes the reliability of the Bible. Can we set the Bible to one side and still extrapolate to a Savior? If God is the creator of all but then stands by dispassionately watching what's going on without intervening, then perhaps not. But what if these things are true: that God made us and made us with moral responsibility, with unique consciousness that mirrors his own; that his consciousness in a mysterious way interacts with ours; that love in the world is not adequately explained except by God's sustaining of it through the generations? If all or even only some of these things are true, then it must also be in God's character to desire reconciliation with the favorites of his creation, when we have torn the relationship asunder.

The relationship was rent by our own perfidy. It doesn't take the fall-of-man story of Genesis for this to be obvious. In the midst of the breathtaking order of the cosmos, there is moral disorder in the heart of mankind. We each have a conscience but no conscience is entirely uncluttered with regrets—moral error that can never be mended. We are conscious not only of our own morally broken selves, but of the brokenness that is ubiquitous

CHAPTER 18: RELIGION

among our kind. It's possible to imagine that this is somehow not the result of broken relationship with One who places moral consciousness on the human heart, but it's a stretch, and if we unimagine God in this transaction, why is there a sense of broken relationship?

If God is not aloof but remains active in the world; if he created us in special relationship to himself; if we have morally broken the world, creating a gap between ourselves and him; and if his justice renders the gap unbridgeable without his own intervention, then does it not stand to reason that he would provide some means of reconciliation? And if he did, what would it look like? We have the advantage of 20/20 hindsight, so we give ourselves too much credit if we say we would have imagined God's reconciliation of us to himself as unfolding in the way of Jesus on earth. Pious Jews of the time pictured a triumphant king who would save the nation of Israel from oppression and defeat her enemies. The Son of David was to be a warrior king who would vindicate God's chosen.

God's way was much larger than Jewish imagination, however. If it had happened that way, Jews would go on living as a special tribe of God's people, but the impact on the world would not have been as it was with Jesus. A military or political triumph would have vindicated God's chosen in the eyes of the world, but it would not have served to reconcile a just God with sinful people. People, including Jews, would have continued on in history living inside a broken relationship with God, without reconciliation.

All people are flawed, living in broken relationship to God, so no mere person could have the heroic stature necessary to reconcile people to God. No sacrifice by a human could ever be adequate to propitiate a just God. No other act of love other than an act of God could accomplish reconciliation without compromising God's justice, and his justice is necessary to the moral authority to which we are, like it or not, subject. The act had to be the death of a person manifesting God, because death is the mark of our humanity. For God to share his spiritual life with us, which is not time-bound, he had to be resurrected. For man to rise from death to be at one with God in timelessness, he has to rise bodily, because he came into life bodily. In order for our identification with Jesus to accomplish these things, he had to have a real birth and die a real death and accomplish a real resurrection. For these things to be effective to people still subject to God's justice, we would thereafter have to identify with Christ, in his death and resurrection. And that would be reflected outwardly, in how we live our lives.

God came into the world of man's cruelty and allowed violent human beings to kill him, so that he could forgive them. The facts of Jesus's Advent, ministry, death, and Resurrection had to unfold in just the way they did, for reconciliation to be possible for those who choose it. Jesus's life, death, and Resurrection were the culmination of the history of the Jews. It was the explosive revelation of God to the other nations. It had to happen the way it did.

The Bible

The whole story is either true or it is not. It comes down to us primarily through the Bible, but in the earliest days following Christ's Ascension it spread by word-of-mouth. In those early days people thought Jesus was coming back imminently. This was a misunderstanding, in the same way people misunderstood the scope of Christ's mission as temporal and immediate, rather than eternal.

People began to write down as faithfully as they could what they witnessed. There was a lot of confusion, frankly, in the early days following Christ's Ascension, and it has taken some time for people to sort it out. It stretches us, especially those of us who live long after the events, trying to make sense of something we haven't experienced first-hand.

The confusion about the truth of the events was not an obstacle early on because so many people saw him after the Resurrection, and experienced first-hand the validation of what Christ taught. The details of a systematic theology were less important to people than knowing they bore witness to the Savior of the world. Coming to understand what Jesus and the pre-Christ scriptures taught about him has been a long-term project.

People are short-term, time-bound thinkers. We piece together evidence to form conclusions, but on a subject as big as this one, we find it difficult to rake all the relevant evidence into our purview. One has to zoom-out, so to speak, to really understood what God was doing in the time of Jesus. The story of the Christ's ministry and Resurrection resonates immediately with some people, but for many the story leaves us scratching our heads. Jesus lived, said things we regard as wise and loving, then was killed because he claimed to be God. Then, according to people who said they knew, he raised himself from the dead and went about showing himself to people to prove the truth of it. Then he bid us good-bye until his return, leaving us

CHAPTER 18: RELIGION

with very general instructions. That's the minimalist version of the story. Even if it is all taken as factually true, what does it mean?

If it is not readily apparent, one has to step back and look at the entirety of the Bible to understand. It's common among Christian Bible-believers to say that Jesus's life and even death and Resurrection were foretold in the Old Testament, in ways he could not have purposely effectuated, therefore the Christian Bible as a whole is in that sense self-proving. That seems to be true because of explicit Old Testament prophecy, such as the oft-cited Isaiah 53, and also by compelling metaphor, as with the Passover Lamb, and countless other events which appear, in retrospect, as obvious advance pictures of the coming Christ.

There is another way in which we can regard the Bible as self-authenticating, and it relates to the Old Testament as a whole. Historical books of the Old Testament are noteworthy for what is excluded as well as what is included. Random-seeming stories are strung together and have valuable lessons, but they also say something to us without explicitly saying it. Here's one example. There are many significant characters in the Old Testament who are in some respect a type of the coming Christ. One of these is Joseph, and he is the subject of many chapters of Genesis. The story of Joseph is interrupted, however, starting at what is now marked chapter 38. That chapter is about Judah, another of the sons of Jacob. We might expect the next chapter to be about other sons of Jacob, but that's not what we get. Following chapter 38, the narrative immediately swerves back into the story of Joseph. Why the interlude about Judah? Why not more on his brothers, too? In the rest of the Old Testament, why stand-alone stories like Ruth and Esther? Why such emphasis on David? Yes, these all tell of the coming Christ, but why these writings and not many other stories of Jewish history which might have been included? It turns out the history books of the Old Testament are ordered on the lineage of Jesus. The super-structure of the Old Testament itself points to the actual Jesus of Nazareth who lived in history. Had the Old Testament canon been generated by Christians, after Christ's Advent, this might have been questionable. But it wasn't. The Old Testament canon was developed by Jewish scholars continuously in the millenia before Christ, and was complete more than 200 years before his Advent.

The Old Testament as a whole teaches several things about the nature and character of God in relation to man that, when rightly understood, point inexorably to a future event more or less like the now-recorded life and ministry of Jesus. These teachings include the love of God, expressed in a personal way, which is why it makes sense that God would work through a particular tribe of people differentiated from the pagan peoples all around them. God's love was manifested to the Hebrews in repeated instances of reconciling himself to them after they pulled away, when they sought temporary earthly things. In the process he refined the character of the Jews in ways still discernible in that people-group to this day. Again and again the tribe God selected evinced a short time-horizon of understanding, falling far short of an eternal perspective. Over time God developed that collective time-horizon to mature this group and make them more disposed to "image" God's perspective of timelessness.

In all of this, the Jews were attempting to reconcile twin pillars of God's character, justice and love, and they were never fully successful at it. The reason was not due to failure of the Jews in particular, but failure of time-bound man in general. God is just and God cannot be not-God. His justice is perfect, just as his love is. That means our moral failing—even one time, in the tiniest conceivable way—separates us from God. God embodies love, and so is merciful to us, but his justice cannot be compromised, else he is not wholly God. We are in conflict with God because of our moral failing.

It would be tempting to think the conflict is God's fault because he made us this way, but thinking that way overlooks the specialness of mankind. This is a feature of mankind that we seem always to be taking for granted: our moral freedom. The cost of our moral freedom is that we have moral accountability. The benefits of our moral freedom are the fullness of our consciousness, in this life, and that we are reconcilable to God.

God's justice and his purity are inseparable in that any moral failing results in separation from him. Because of man's moral awareness, separation from God is hell. In this life we can repudiate God and still enjoy the benefits of his common grace on mankind—the rain falls on the just and the unjust alike—but this state ends when life in this body ends. Our moral awareness remains, but does so in a state of separation from God if we are not reconciled to him.

Man cannot reconcile himself to God. We don't have the moral purity required. The enmity with God remains, if it is up to mankind to bridge the gap. Thankfully, it is bridged by God himself. As an instance of his love, he accomplishes the reconciliation. As an instance of his justice, he bears the utter separation in the person of the Christ. This transaction took place physically in the crucifixion. Exactly how it takes place spiritually is beyond our understanding now, but it does make sense that perfect justice requires perfect love, and love must be manifested in sacrifice, to be complete. Jesus acted out of perfect love, and perfect justice required his sacrifice. It was all at God's initiative. He loved first, and acted on his love unilaterally, just as in the ceremony wherein he expressed his covenant with Abraham in Genesis 15. Parties to a contract would solemnize their promises by walking together between the parts of slaughtered animals. On that occasion, though, God did it alone. God reaches to us unilaterally.

To grasp how this all works we delve into the Trinity, an understanding of God in three "persons," each a manifestation of the one God but in different roles, God the just father; Jesus the obedient man-God incarnated; and the Holy Spirit as present in the world. The relationship among the three persons of the trinity is helpful to us in making sense of this divine transaction necessary to reconcile God to his people. Apart from this basic proposition, however, we speculate into the nature of something so far beyond us that we in this life must grope about with tenuous clues about the ineffable nature of God Almighty, maker of heaven and earth.

Chapter 19: **Silence**

JESUS DIED AND THEN was resurrected, and then went about showing himself to people so they would see he was resurrected, and by extension so would be all those who were "in him," meaning identifying with him in some way more significant than merely saying so. After that he ascended, in an unmistakably significant way. And then: silence. For something like 2000 years and counting. Jesus's followers preached Jesus's imminent return, but he did not return in their lifetimes as anticipated. At this writing, he has not yet returned.

From time to time, people who look for him say he is coming now or at a certain time in the future, but it so far hasn't happened. He told his followers while among us bodily that the precise time of his returning could not be anticipated specifically. But should it take this long? And why? What are we supposed to be doing in this interregnum?

We should not look at the time from Christ's Ascension to now as being dead time, historically. God has a plan to be worked out in history. We can see it fairly clearly in the Old Testament because there is a historical record of the working out of God's relationship to his people. You might say it was a lesson in long-term training by God. History didn't end with the Advent of the Christ. It is reasonable to conclude that the time from then to now is part of God's plan for his people. There is no reason to discard the idea of a *telos* built into the unfolding of history, even after Jesus was resurrected. Exactly how makes for some speculation, though we could perhaps trace God's likely purposes in the development of the Christian churches and the civilizations that have evolved with Christian understanding, down to the present day when that understanding withers in the places it was once vibrant, leaving a remnant of a faithful few. It's not clear to us why history is unfolding the way it is now; we don't have the playbook written with hindsight, as with the Old Testament. But it stands to reason that God has his hand on the direction of history, and it's a worthwhile endeavor to try to discern where he is taking us.

CHAPTER 19: SILENCE

Still, for now it feels like silence, if we disregard the elements of God's presence in the world which we are privileged to be able to take for granted. Silence is a dead weight on the souls of mankind. We wait. We observe all around us circumstances we deem sufficient to warrant his imminent return, but he doesn't show. We scour the scriptures for clues as to when all things will be made new. But old things continue in their downward spiral. Maybe it was all a dream? Was it only wishful thinking handed down from Christ-believing Jews of the first century?

It's in our nature to live as though we will live forever, though we know the mortality rate is 100 percent. We tend not to see our own lives as sparks that fly upward in the night, fireflies against the night sky, extinguishing up there somewhere and falling to earth as gray ash. But that's what we are, apart from the soul. If we had been born during Jesus's lifetime, maybe we'd have encountered him, and have seen him for who he is. But maybe we'd have seen him as just another good teacher, like many of his followers did, until after the Resurrection. Or maybe we'd not meet him at all, being far from the crucible of civilization in which he directly ministered. And yet, people encounter Jesus now and in every age since his Advent, at different times and different places. We encounter Jesus today as surely as people did when he conducted his earthly ministry.

We must better understand the nature of the God we are talking about. Jesus hasn't returned, but Jesus is a part of the three-fold person of God, and God has not been absent. God's active, current presence is manifested in the existence of physical things, including human beings. The beauty in the world screams his existence; he is not silent. In fact, existence *of anything* screams God's existence, because there simply had to be a higher, immaterial cause for material things. Stuff does not create itself.

But let's suppose that this doesn't qualify as breaking the silence, for some reason. God could adopt a tribe, and perform great miracles among them, taking them in a direction contrary to the pagan tendencies of all the people groups around them, and demonstrate in countless ways his repeated return to those people despite their faithlessness to him. And all the while, he could promise them a coming savior who would bridge the gap that he disclosed between his righteousness, and the depravity of every living human.

Still not enough? Still too quiet? What would God have to do, to tell us he is, and not be regarded as "silent?" Well, he could manifest himself in the world in some tangible way. And while he's at it, he could do it in a way that would be recognizable to us, such as appearing among us as a person. And while he's at that, he could show us the qualities to which we should aspire. And he could not only appear himself, but do things that are impossible to do, unless there is a greater spiritual reality beyond what we see. He could perform miracles that are explicable only if there is a spiritual realm, say. Even raise someone from the dead. Even raise his own human form from the dead. How about that? Would that do it? Does that break the silence? How about if he uses this event to reconcile his purity with our impurity; his justice with his own mercy? He could allow us to humiliate and spit upon him but go to his death anyway, before giving us his final proof. How about that? Does that still count as silence?

Well. That was long ago. Maybe it wasn't even real. Maybe it's just a story told by a bunch of over-excited credulous bumpkins. But maybe we go to the opposite extreme, unwilling to believe anything remotely out of the ordinary. Some people could have a live, visual manifestation right in front of them, and that would count as silence, too. It would be chalked up to psychological hallucination or something. Truly, if one does not listen to the prophets of old, they will not be convinced even if someone rises from the dead. (Luke 16:31). One day the truth will be obvious to everyone (Romans 14:11) but that day is not this day.

The problem isn't God's silence, it's our refusal to listen. We listen if we have a fear of the Lord, and he calls us to it or he doesn't. It's his prerogative, we don't second-guess God. Every day of delay should be credited to God's patience. We should nonetheless be mindful that every day that passes brings us closer to the day of the Lord.

What's happening isn't silence. Love is present in the world, and that is the Spirit of God. The orientations to the good, the true, and the beautiful are within the Spirit of God. The force of life expressed in regeneration down through the years—that is of God, too. The consciousness of God mingles mysteriously with the consciousness of man because we are made in his image. That evidences the presence of God with us still today. We have an intuition of the presence of God, if we do not purposely squelch it. That intuition is a soft, still voice whispering to us; to people from generation to generation from that day to this. Our job is to hear. Cultivating this sense of his presence takes some effort, and an open-heartedness to the prospect that he is. Then the assurance of his presence follows. That's what faith is—not "believing what we know ain't so," (Mark Twain) but "the assurance of things hoped for, the conviction of things not seen." (Hebrews 11).

CHAPTER 19: SILENCE

We perceive the silence broken when we understand that the love we experience and show others in the world comes from God. Love is the spirit of God in the world. It is not something we see or hear, except in its effects, in the same way we "see" wind because it riffles the leaves. It is something we feel, and that feeling has no adequate explanation in materialism, the chief spirit of delusion of this age.

THE END

Bibliography

Abbott, Edwin Abbott. *Flatland: A Romance of Many Dimensions*. London: Seeley & Co. 1884.

Augros, Michael. *Who Designed the Designer?/A Rediscovered Path to God's Existence*. San Francisco: Ignatius 2015.

Augros, Robert and George Stanciu. *The New Story of Science*. New York: Bantam 1984.

Baker, Hunter. *The End of Secularism*. Wheaton, IL: Crossway 2009.

Baldwin, J.F. *The Deadliest Monster/An Introduction to Worldviews*. New Brunfels, TX: Fishermen 2005 (4th ed.).

Behe, Michael J. *Darwin's Black Box/The Biochemical Challenge to Evolution*. New York: Free Press 1996.

Boa, Kenneth. *Conformed to His Image/Biblical and Practical Approaches to Spiritual Formation*. Grand Rapids, MI: Zondervan 2001.

Boa, Kenneth D. and Robert M. Bowman, Jr. *20 Compelling Evidences that God Exists/Discover Why Believing in God Makes So Much Sense*. Tulsa, OK: River Oak 2002.

Boa, Ken and Larry Moody. *I'm Glad You Asked/In-depth Answers to Questions about Christianity*. Colorado Springs: Victor 2005.

Boethius, Ancius. *Consolation of Philosophy*. New York: Penguin 1982.

Bloom, Harold. *The American Religion*. New York: Chu Hartley 2006 (2nd ed.).

Budziszewski, J. *Written on the Heart/The Case for Natural Law*. Downers Grove, IL: Intervarsity 1997.

Camus, Albert. *The Myth of Sisyphus and Other Essays*. London: H. Hamilton 1965.

Carroll, Sean. *The Big Picture/On the Origin of Life, Meaning, and the Universe Itself*. New York: Dutton 2016.

Clegg, Brian. *The God Effect/Quantum Entanglement, Science's Strongest Phenomenon*. New York: St. Martin's 2006.

Clouser, Roy A. *The Myth of Religious Neutrality/An Essay on the Hidden Role of Religious Belief in Theories*. Notre Dame: University of Notre Dame Press 2006.

Colling, Richard G. *Random Designer/Created From Chaos to Connect with the Creator*. Bourbonnais, IL: Browning 2004.

Darwin, Charles. *On the Origin of Species*. London: John Murray 1859.

Davies, Paul. *The Mind of God/The Scientific Basis for a Rational World*. New York: Simon & Shuster 1992.

Dawkins, Richard. *The God Delusion*. New York: Houghton Mifflin 2006.

———. *The Greatest Show on Earth/The Evidence for Evolution*. New York: Free Press 2009.
Dennett, Daniel C. *Breaking the Spell/Religion as a Natural Phenomenon*. New York: Penguin 2006.
———. *Darwin's Dangerous Idea/Evolution and the Meanings of Life*. New York: Simon & Schuster 1995.
Dewey, John. *A Common Faith*. New Haven, CT: Yale University Press 1934.
Dostoyevsky, Fyodor. *Crime and Punishment*. New York: Collier & Son 1917.
Durkheim, Emile. *The Elementary Forms of the Religious Life*. New York: Macmillan 1915.
Dworkin, Ronald. *Religion Without God*. Cambridge, MA: Harvard University Press 2013.
Dyson, Freeman. *Disturbing the Universe*. New York: Harper & Row 1979.
Feser, Edward. *The Last Supersititon/A Refutation of the New Atheism*. South Bend, IN: St. Augustine's 2008.
———. *Philosophy of Mind*. London: Oneworld 2005.
Flew, Anthony. *There is a God/How the World's Most Notorious Atheist Changed His Mind*. New York: HarperOne 2007.
Geisler, Norman L. and Frank Turek. *I Don't Have Enough Faith to be an Atheist*. Wheaton, IL: Crossway 2004.
Geisler, Norman L. and Patrick Zukeran. *Christian Apologetics*. Grand Rapids, MI: Baker 2009.
Gabriel, Markus. *I Am Not a Brain*. Medford, MA: Polity Press 2017.
Gilbert, Alan D. *The Making of Post-Christian Britain/A History of the Secularization of Modern Society*. New York: Longman 1980.
Grayling, A.C. *The God Argument/The Case Against Religion and for Humanism*. New York: Bloomsbury USA 2013.
Gribbin, John. *The Birth of Time/How Astronomers Measured the Age of the Universe*. New Haven, CT: Yale University Press 1999.
Girard, Rene. *I See Satan Fall Like Lightning*. Maryknoll, NY: Orbis 2001.
———. *Things Hidden Since the Foundation of the World*. Stanford, CA: Stanford University Press 1987.
Harris, Sam. *Letter to A Christian Nation*. New York: Vintage 2006.
Hart, David Bentley. *Atheist Delusions/The Christian Revolution and Its Fashionable Enemies*. New Haven: Yale University Press 2009.
———. *The Experience of God/Being, Consciousness, Bliss*. New Haven, CT: Yale University Press 2013.
———. *The Story of Christianity/A History of 2000 Years of the Christian Faith*. London: Quercus Editions 2009.
Hasker, William. *The Emergent Self*. Ithaca, NY: Cornell University Press 1999.
Hicks, Stephen R.C. *Explaining Postmodernism/Skepticism and Socialism From Rousseau to Foucault*. Ockham's Razor 2017 (3rd ed.).
Hitchens, Christopher. *God is Not Great/How Religion Poisons Everything*. New York: Twelve 2009.
Hitchens, Peter. *The Rage Against God*. London: Continuum 2010.
Howard, Thomas. *Chance or the Dance/A Critique of Modern Secularism*. San Francisco: Ignatius 1969.
Jacoby, Susan. *Freethinkers/A History of American Secularism*. New York: Owl 2004.
James, William. *Will to Believe*. New York: Dover 1956.

BIBLIOGRAPHY

Keller, Timothy. *The Reason for God/Belief in an Age of Skepticism.* New York: Dutton 2008.
Krauss, Lawrence M. *A Universe from Nothing/Why There is Something Rather than Nothing.* New York: Atria 2012.
Kundera, Milan. *The Unbearable Lightness of Being.* New York: Harper & Row 1984.
Lewis, C.S. *God in the Dock.* Grand Rapids, MI: Eerdman's 2002.
Koukl, Gregory. *The Story of Reality/How the World Began, How it Ends, and Everything Important that Happens in Between.* Grand Rapids, MI: Zondervan 2017.
Larson, Edward. *Summer for the Gods/The Scopes Trial and America's Continuing Debate Over Science and Religion.* New York: BasicBooks 1997.
Ledewitz, Bruce. *Church, State, and the Crisis in American Secularism.* Bloomington: Indiana University Press 2011.
Lennox, John. *God's Undertaker/Has Science Buried God?* Oxford, England: Lion 2009.
Lewis, C.S. *The Abolition of Man.* New York: HarperOne 2000.
———. *Mere Christianity.* New York: Macmillan 1960.
Lewis, C.S. and Joy Davidman. *Miracles: A Preliminary Study.* 1947.
McDowell, Josh. *The New Evidence that Demands a Verdict.* Tenn: Thomas Nelson 1999.
MacIntyre, Alisdair. *After Virtue.* Notre Dame, IN: University of Notre Dame Press 1984 (2nd ed.)
Makari, George. *Soul Machine/The Invention of the Modern Mind.* New York: Norton 2015.
Mayr, Ernest. *What Evolution Is.* New York: Perseus 2001.
Merrick, Trenton. *Truth and Ontology.* Oxford: Oxford University Press 2009.
Noll, Mark A. *The Scandal of the Evangelical Mind.* Grand Rapids, MI: Eerdmans 1994.
Otto, Rudolf. *The Idea of the Holy.* London: Oxford University Press 1950 (2nd ed.)
Plantinga, Alvin. *Knowledge and Christian Belief.* Grand Rapids, MI: Eerdman's 2015.
Rorty, Richard and Gianni Vattimo. *The Future of Religion.* New York: Columbia University Press 2004.
Ridley, Matt. *The Evolution of Everything/How New Ideas Emerge.* New York: HarperCollins 2015.
Ruse, Michael. *Darwinism As Religion/What Literature Tells Us about Evolution.* New York: Oxford University Press 2017.
Sacks, Jonathan. *Not in God's Name.* New York: Schocken 2015.
Schaeffer, Francis A. *The God Who is There.* Downers Grove, IL: Intervarsity 1968.
Schroeder, Gerald. *The Science of God/The Convergence of Scientific and Biblical Wisdom..* New York: The Free Press 1997.
Schutt, Michael P. *Redeeming Law/Christian Calling and the Legal Profession.* Downers Grove, IL: Intervarsity 2007.
Scruton, Roger. *Beauty/A Very Short Introduction.* New York: Oxford University Press 2011.
———. *Modern Philosophy/An Introduction and Survey.* New York: Penguin 1994.
———. *The Soul of the World.* Princeton, NJ: Princeton University Press 2014.
Scruton, Roger and Peter Singer and Christopher Ganaway and Michael Tanner. *German Philosophers, Kant, Hegel, Schopenhauer, and Nietzsche.* New York: Oxford University Press 1997.
Seidentop, Larry. *Inventing the Individual/The Origins of Western Liberalism.* Cambridge, MA: Belknap 2014.
Sire, James W., *The Universe Next Door/A Basic Worldview Catalog.* Downers Grove, IL: Intervarsity 1997 (3rd ed.).

Skeel, David. *True Paradox/How Christianity Makes Sense of Our Complex World*. Downers Grove, IL: Intervarsity 2014.
Smith, James K.A. *How (Not) to be Secular/Reading Charles Taylor*. Grand Rapids, MI: Eerdman's 2014.
Smith, Steven D. *The Disenchantment of Secular Discourse*. Cambridge, MA: Harvard University Press 2010.
———. *Foreordained Failure/The Quest for a Constititutional Principle of Religious Freedom*. New York: Oxford University Press 1995.
———. *Pagans & Christians in the City/Culture Wars from the Tiber to the Potomac*. Grand Rapids, MI: Eerdman's 2018.
Stenger, Victor J. *God/The Failed Hypothesis/How Science Shows That God Does Not Exist*. Amherst, NY: Prometheus 2007.
Strobel, Lee. *The Case for Christ/A Journalist's Personal Investigation of the Evidence for Jesus*. Grand Rapids, MI: Zondervan 1998.
Taylor, Charles. *A Secular Age*. Cambridge, MA: Belknap 2007.
Tipler, Frank J. *The Physics of Christianity*. New York: Doubleday 2007.
———. *The Physics of Immortality*. New York: Doubleday 1994.
Vardy, Peter. *An Introduction to Kierkegaard*. Peabody, MA: Penguin 2008.
Wallace, J. Warner, *Cold Case Christianity*. Colorado Springs: David C. Cook 2019.
Walton, John H. *The Lost World of Genesis One/Ancient Cosmology and the Origins Debate*. Downers Grove, IL: Intervarsity 2009.
Weber, Max. *The Sociology of Religion*. Boston, MA: 1922 (2nd ed.).
Williams, Rowan. *On Being Human/Bodies, Minds, Persons*. Grand Rapids, MI: Eerdman's 2018.
Wills, Garry. *Head and Heart/America Christianities*. New York: Penguin 2007.
Wordsworth, William. *Poems, In Two Volumes*. 1804.
Zacharias, Ravi. *The End of Reason/A Response to the New Atheists*. Grand Rapids, MI: Zondervan 2008.
Zuckerman, Phil. *Living the Secular Life/New Answers to Old Questions*. New York: Penguin 2014.

www.ingramcontent.com/pod-product-compliance
Lightning Source LLC
Chambersburg PA
CBHW060823190426
43197CB00038B/2203